The Salon Doré

DARE MYERS HARTWELL

with essays by

BRUNO PONS

ANDRÉ BAEYENS

Introduction by

JACK COWART

THE CORCORAN GALLERY OF ART, WASHINGTON, D.C.

1998

Editor

Nancy Eickel

Designer

Timothy B. Connor

Printer

Balding + Mansell Limited

Printed and bound in

England

Cover

Detail of the Salon Doré trophy panel depicting Love.

Title page, plate 1

Detail of the Salon Doré trophy panel depicting Victory.

Library of Congress Cataloging-in-Publication Data

Corcoran Gallery of Art.

    The Salon Doré / Dare Myers Hartwell ; with essays by Bruno Pons,

André Baeyens ; introduction by Jack Cowart.

      p. cm.

    Includes bibliographical references.

    ISBN 0-88675-055-5 (pbk. : alk. paper)

     1. Salon Doré. 2. Neoclassicism (Architecture)—France.

3. Decoration and ornament—France—Neoclassicism. 4. Interior

architecture—France—Conservation and restoration. 5. Corcoran

Gallery of Art. I. Hartwell, Dare Myers. II. Pons, Bruno.

III. Baeyens, André. IV. Title.

NA2854.C67 1998   98-4628

747.7'50944'09033—dc21   CIP

CONTENTS

FACING PAGE

PLATE 2

Detail of the Salon Doré trophy panel depicting Music.

THE CORCORAN GALLERY OF ART

*gratefully acknowledges the generosity of the following major donors
to the restoration of the Salon Doré:*

Anonymous

The Morris and Gwendolyn Cafritz Foundation

The Getty Grant Program

The Florence Gould Foundation

In memory of Constance B. Mellon - by her family

Air France

Ella Poe Burling

Lee and Juliet Folger

The Folger Fund

Friends of French Art

Friends of Vieilles Maisons Françaises in honor of
        Ambassador Emmanuel de Margerie and Madame de Margerie

Mr. and Mrs. John H. Hall, Jr.

National Endowment for the Arts

George Parker, Jr.

The Marjorie Merriweather Post Foundation

Prince Charitable Trusts

Joseph E. Seagram & Sons, Inc.

Société Général

Sotheby's

The Women's Committee of the Corcoran Gallery of Art

This publication was made possible by generous grants from the
Samuel H. Kress Foundation and an anonymous donor, with
additional funding from Mr. and Mrs. John H. Hall, Jr., and support from
the Corcoran's Andrew W. Mellon Research and Publications Fund
and the Kathrine Dulin Folger Publications Fund.

The Corcoran has established The Salon Doré Fund to accept donations
reserved for the acquisition of historic furnishings and for other projects
essential to the preservation and interpretation of the Salon.

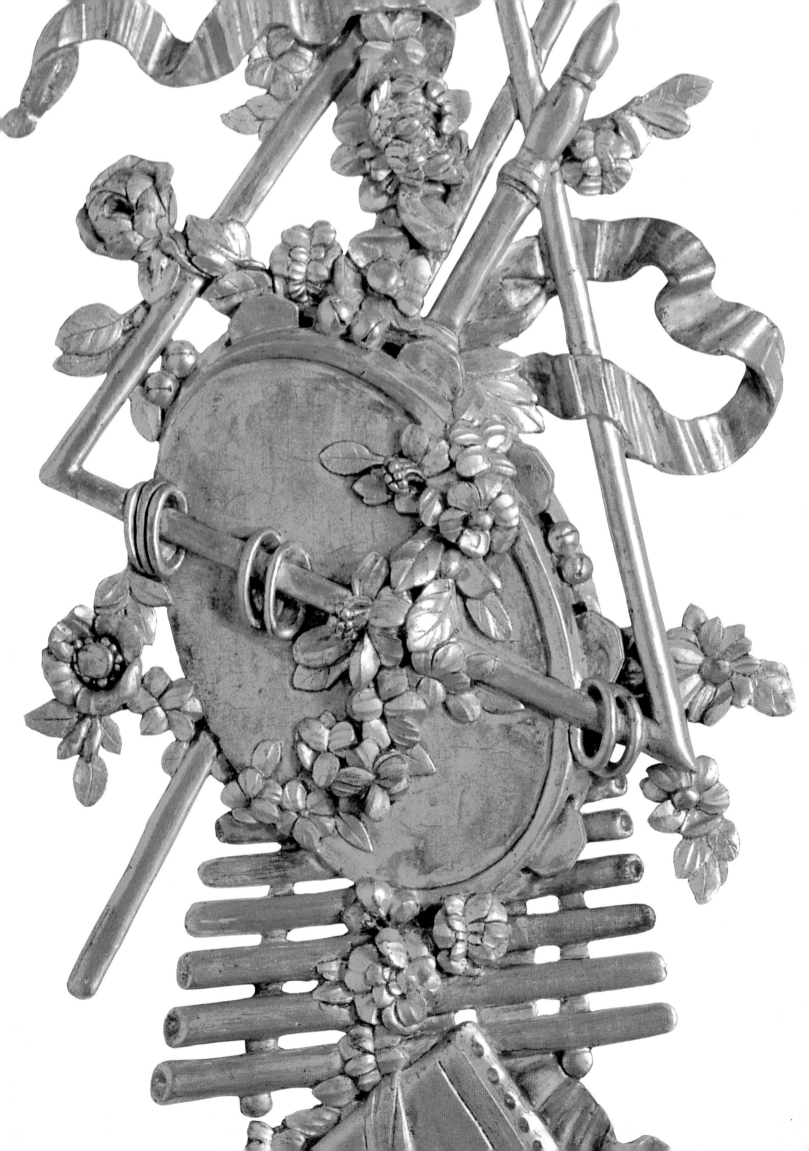

INTRODUCTION
Paris - New York - Washington

JACK COWART

This collection of essays presents the results of research conducted in preparation for, and deriving from, the major restoration of the Salon Doré (or gilded room), the unique eighteenth-century French room now in the Corcoran Gallery of Art. Study of the room began in 1987, the restoration took place from 1989 to 1993, and research and writing continued well into 1996. From its origins in Paris in 1770 to today, the room's wonderful mirrored, carved, and gilded *boiserie* (wood paneling) and its ceiling mural have endured a fascinating odyssey. Beginning as a relatively square *salon de compagnie* (room for receiving guests) in a distinguished pre-Revolutionary Parisian private residence called the hôtel de Clermont, it was expanded at the beginning of this century into a longer rectangle and re-used as the "grand salon" in Senator William Andrews Clark's mansion on Fifth Avenue in New York. Subsequently reinstalled as a theatrical "period room" at the Corcoran in 1927, the recent restoration returned the surfaces (if not the structure) of the Salon Doré as much as possible to their eighteenth-century appearance and opened up the room to visitors, allowing the artistry of the carving and gilding to be viewed at close range as was originally intended. Although in its beauty of design and craftsmanship the Salon Doré needs no explanation, it is our intent here to put the room in context and to increase public understanding and appreciation for what is arguably the finest *boiserie* in the United States.

The hôtel de Clermont, located at 69, rue de Varenne, in the faubourg Saint-Germain area of Paris, was built at the beginning of the eighteenth century for the Marquise de Saissac, a widow whose husband's family name was Clermont. The term *hôtel* implies *hôtel particulier,* a large private residence. The hotel's architect was the well-known Jean-Baptiste-Alexandre Le Blond (1679–1719). It became known as the hôtel d'Orsay after it was purchased in 1768 by the comte (count) d'Orsay, who almost immediately commissioned the creation of the Salon Doré in an existing ground floor room. Over the centuries, the name of the house changed with successive owners, but when it was transferred to the French state in 1944 by the heirs of the last private owner, Eugène Aubrey-Vitet, the French government reinstated the original name of hôtel de Clermont.[1] As the tenure of the comte d'Orsay was perhaps the hôtel's most glorious period, and certainly the one with which the Salon Doré is most intimately associated, we have chosen to reconnect our room to its historic roots and maintain the name of hôtel d'Orsay in the following articles (particularly since, to make matters even more confusing, this name continues to be used by French experts in eighteenth-century decorative arts).

In his article on the Parisian origins of the Salon Doré, Bruno Pons describes the development of the vast and beautiful mansions in the faubourg Saint-Germain at the beginning of the eighteenth century. Today, like many other of these mansions, the hôtel de Clermont houses offices of various ministries of the French government, including the Ministry of Communication. Directly across the street, at 78, rue de Varenne, stands the hôtel de Villeroy, presently the location of the Ministry of Agriculture and Fishing, and one block to the east, at 57, rue de Varenne, is the hôtel Matignon, office of the prime minister. The hôtel de Boisgelin at 47, rue de Varenne is now the Italian embassy, representing another frequent use for these ancient hôtels. At the west end of the street, along the Boulevard des Invalides, is the Musée Rodin, formerly the hôtel Biron. On the rue de Grenelle, which runs parallel to the rue de Varenne, eighteenth-century hôtels house the Ministry of Work, Employment, and Professional Training, the Ministry of Education, the municipal building for the seventh *arrondissement* (district), and the Swiss and Korean embassies. Today the extensive gardens that once separated these hôtels are densely packed with buildings containing apartments, small hotels, specialty shops, and restaurants. With the exception of a few large boulevards, the streets are narrow and generally run one way. Policemen stand guard to provide protection for the ministries.

The west end of the rue de Varenne is bordered by the hôtel des Invalides and its esplanade, which reaches to the Seine. Originally built by Louis XIV for retired soldiers, the building now houses the Army Museum, the museum of the Order of Liberation, and two churches, the Église Saint-Louis and the Église du Dôme. The latter is surmounted by the famous dome that has become one of the landmarks of the Paris skyline. Designed by Jules Hardouin Mansart (1646–1708), the favorite architect of Louis XIV, its lead covering is decorated with gilded military trophies.[2] Directly under the dome lies the tomb of Napoleon. Coincidentally, the Dome of the Invalides was recently regilded by the ateliers Gohard, which also carried out the restoration of the gilded paneling in the Salon Doré.

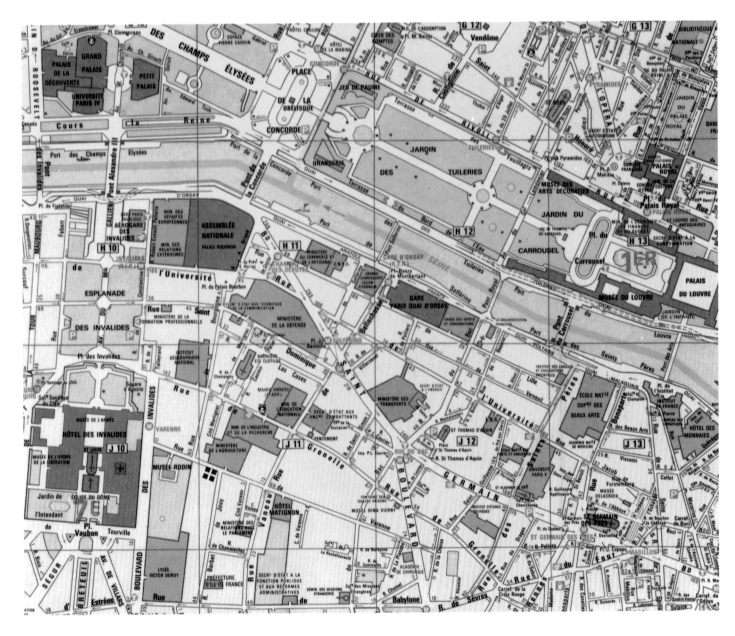

FIGURE 1

Map of the faubourg Saint-Germain, Paris. © MICHE-
LIN *after Paris Plan No. 20 (1977). Permission No.
9708420P. The hôtel de Clermont is at the intersection of rue
de Varenne and rue Barbet de Jouy.*

The Boulevard Saint-Germain now runs between the rue de Varenne and the Seine.
On it stands the old abbey church of Saint-Germain des Prés (Saint-Germain in the
Fields), which gave its name to this formerly bucolic neighborhood. Today it shares a
busy city street with boutiques of clothing by leading fashion designers, stores offering
upscale furnishings, restaurants, and two of the most famous cafés in Paris, Les Deux
Magots and Flore. These two cafés, along with the almost equally famous *brasserie* Lipp
across the street, have been in business for more than a century. Café Flore is at present
the more fashionable, but in earlier times Oscar Wilde, James Joyce, and Ernest
Hemingway were all *habitués* of Les Deux Magots, and it was made legendary by Albert
Camus, Jean-Paul Sartre, and Simone de Beauvoir. This then is the neighborhood of the
hôtel de Clermont today, a combination of the conventional and the colorful. Historic,
elegant, and staid, it also abounds in the bustling street life that has come to characterize
contemporary Paris.

We do not know why the Duchâtel family, the nineteenth-century owners of the
house, decided to sell the eighteenth-century paneling and ceiling murals on the ground

II

FIGURE 2

Hôtel de Clermont, present day from the rue de Varenne.

floor. Conventional reasons—financial necessity or a desire for something more contemporary—do not seem to apply. The family is still economically secure, and curiously, the original Salon Doré paneling was replaced with a replica cast in plaster at the time of its removal.

This plaster cast caused some confusion at the beginning of our research. A well-known series of books published in the early twentieth century by F. Contet on the hôtels of the old districts of Paris features two detailed photographs of the Salon Doré in the "hôtel d'Orsay." [3] When these photographs were compared to the Corcoran's room, minor but significant differences became apparent, for example, in the detailing of the garlands between the pilaster capitals, in the flowers painted on the doors, and in the curious repetition of a trophy panel, seen in one photograph reflected in the mirror over the mantel. All of this suggested that ours might not be the fabled Salon Doré of the comte d'Orsay. Our concerns were put to rest, however, when we found that the furnishings in the photograph belonged to Monsieur and Madame Aubrey-Vitet, who had purchased the hôtel in 1905 after the Salon Doré had been sold to Senator Clark. It then became obvious that the "Salon Doré" illustrated by Contet was in fact the plaster copy. Subsequent visits to the hôtel de Clermont by Bruno Pons, Christian Prévost-Marcilhacy, Inspecteur Général des Monuments Historiques, and the Corcoran team responsible for the restoration made it clear that the Corcoran possesses the majority of the paneling from the original room. Most of what remains in the hôtel de Clermont is an obvious, but evocative, replication in plaster.

It should also be noted that the treatment of the pilasters is different in the two rooms: the original pilasters are completely gilded whereas the plaster copies are only partially gilded. Again, this caused confusion at the beginning of our research since it is a natural assumption that the copy would follow the original. In fact, the partial gilding reflects a *fin-de-siécle* sensibility and not the appearance of the original pilasters before their sale.

The Salon Doré, with its Corinthian pilasters, formal clarity, and symmetry, epitomizes the early neoclassical style. In its rejection of the curvilinear ambiguity of the rococo, the dominant style in France in the first part of the eighteenth century, neoclassicism returned to the forms of classical antiquity inspired in part by the excavations at Herculaneum (from 1738) and Pompeii (from 1748). Although the comte d'Orsay did not actually visit Italy until five years after the Salon Doré was completed, his interest in antiquity was fostered at an early age by his mother's marriage to a poet and translator of Greek tragedies. During the count's Italian sojourn (1775–78), he accompanied scholars on archeological excavations, studied antique monuments, and amassed an extensive collection of objects, some genuinely antique and others copies after the antique.[4] The alabaster for the tops of the pier tables commissioned for the Salon Doré was most likely removed from an antique monument.[5] In his advocacy of the neoclassical style, the comte d'Orsay's taste was both avant-garde and influential.

The Salon Doré came to the Corcoran Gallery in 1926 as part of the bequest of Senator William Andrews Clark. Born near Connellsville, Pennsylvania, on 8 January 1839, Clark and his family moved to Iowa in 1856. Six years later, at the age of twenty-three, he went west to work as a miner. Clark eventually settled in Montana, where he established wholesale goods and banking businesses in several mining towns. By 1872, at the age of thirty-three, he was "the leading banker, merchant and capitalist in the Territory of Montana."[6] To further his mining and mineralogical knowledge, he went to New York in 1872 and 1873 to study at Columbia University's School of Mines. He began to purchase controlling interests in silver and copper mines, initially in Montana, but in time throughout the West and in the East as well. His most profitable mine was the United Verde Copper Company in Arizona, and Clark soon became known as one of the "copper kings" of America.

Always interested in politics, Clark ran for senator several times, and in 1901 he was finally elected by the Montana legislature. About this time construction of his magnificent house in New York began, and the Salon Doré was purchased to be its "grand salon." (Dare Myers Hartwell describes the house in detail in her article.) Clark served only one term in the United States Senate and then returned to New York.

Senator Clark's art collecting seems to have commenced in earnest about the time he began planning his New York residence, and it was undoubtedly connected to his need to fill its hundred-plus rooms. Not unlike his contemporary American industrialists, his taste in art was conservative. He bought Old Master paintings and drawings, English portraits, and works by nineteenth-century French painters of the Barbizon school; Gothic, Beauvais, and Gobelins tapestries; Indo-European rugs; French, Flemish, Italian, and Venetian lace; Greek and Roman antiquities ranging from the eighth to the second century B.C.; Italian Renaissance maiolica, Delft and Palissy ware; and European sculpture, furniture, and decorative objects. His collecting should be viewed with that of the other great capitalists of his era—J. P. Morgan, Henry Clay Frick, Andrew Carnegie, and Peter A. B. Widener, to name only a few of the most prominent men who were forming their own encyclopedic collections. For them, European art was a social caché representing both a belief in continental values and sophistication, and the romantic lure of an older culture with a grander history.

Senator Clark purchased works of art both singly and *en masse*. He bought from well-known international dealers, auction houses in New York, and occasionally individual collectors and artists. His antiquities were purchased as a group from Raphael Collin, a Paris artist who had worked with experts at the Louvre to assemble a collection of terra-cotta figures, vases, and architectural elements. (Collin also painted the murals in the "petit salon" in Senator Clark's house.)[7] The maiolica was bought from the Hanaure estate in Berlin and the Garet collection in Paris. Most of the Old Master paintings came from the collections of Sir George Donaldson in London and Gottfried von Preyer in Vienna.

It has been said that Clark, as a dilettante, formed his collection by acquiring what appealed to him. Even though he lacked a historical program or consistent advice from specialists, he bought well. The European paintings and decorative arts that he bequeathed to the Corcoran are among the cornerstones of the museum's collection, and the majority of the objects retain their national and international importance as works of considerable quality.

The Salon Doré as we know it today is the product of two great patrons of the arts, the French comte d'Orsay and the Francophile Senator Clark. While the reader will learn more about the count and the impact of the senator on the Salon Doré in the articles that follow, it should be said now that quintessential similarities define the lives of these two men, even though one was an eighteenth-century Frenchman born to wealth and privilege and the other was a nineteenth-century self-made American industrialist. They are linked across the ages as passionate collectors of the antique and the Old World, who at the same time used art and architecture to foster their social ambitions. Both were unrivaled *amateurs* of the arts and enlightened spirits who encouraged the advance of knowledge, culture, and civilization. This publication salutes the vision of these collectors who were born ninety-one years and two worlds apart.

In the present day there are many whose interest and generosity have significantly affected the Salon Doré and who deserve our profound personal and institutional gratitude. Foremost among these are Juliet Folger and the Women's Committee of the Corcoran Gallery of Art, who were among the first supporters of the restoration of the room, providing initiative, enthusiasm, and financial support. Now led by Elaine Silverstein, the Salon Doré Committee of the Women's Committee continues its vital advocacy of this historic room.

The early commitment to the project of Emmanuel de Margerie, French ambassador to the United States, and Madame de Margerie provided access to invaluable expertise and advice, and their support was continued by their successors, Ambassador and Madame Jacques Andréani. Catherine de Logères of the Ministry of Trade and Artisans worked tirelessly to aid us in our research and in the selection of the ateliers Gohard to restore the gilded paneling. The efforts of the Corcoran's executive directors, senior staff, and Leonard Silverstein were critical to our fundraising efforts.

Christian Prévost-Marcilhacy, Inspecteur Général des Monuments Historiques, guided us throughout the restoration, and Christian Baulez, Conservateur en Chef, Musée National des châteaux de Versailles et de Trianon, furnished invaluable information on the hôtel de Clermont. Many others in France were also generous with their knowledge, most notably, Daniel Meyer, Conservateur en Chef, Musée National des châteaux de Versailles et de Trianon; Jean Nérée Ronfort; Jean-Dominique Augarde; and the Ministry of Culture. Brigitte Gournay and Marie-Christine Vigutto helped prepare Bruno Pons's manuscript for publication. Nadine Gasc, Conservateur en Chef, Musée des arts décoratifs, allowed us to cast a replacement flame for our "vestals" clock from their slightly earlier version. To commemorate the restoration, Hèrmes of Paris, Inc., designed a scarf that is sold exclusively in the Corcoran Shop. At the French embassy in Washington, we are grateful for the aid of Anne Lewis-Loubignac, Cultural Attaché during the restoration; Bernard Braem, her successor; and Megan Allday.

At the J. Paul Getty Museum, Gillian Wilson, Curator of Decorative Arts, and Brian B. Considine, Conservator of Decorative Arts and Sculpture, gave us essential advice throughout the project. Paul Miller, Associate Curator of the Preservation Society of Newport County (Newport, Rhode Island), generously shared his research on the Paris decorating house of Jules Allard and Sons. At the National Gallery of Art, we are indebted to Ross Merrill, Chief of Conservation; René de la Rie, Head of the Scientific Research Department; Barbara Berrie, Senior Conservation Scientist; and Stephan Wilcox, Frame Conservator. Curator of Northern Renaissance Art John Hand also provided invaluable assistance and counsel. Ray Seefeldt, International Exchange Officer of the Smithsonian Institution, arranged visas for the French artisans.

The restoration of the Salon Doré would not have been possible without the support of each department of the Corcoran Gallery. We would like to thank several people specifically, including former staff members Edward Nygren, Curator of Collections in the initial stages of the project; Franklin Kelly, Curator of Collections 1988–90; and William Bodine, Assistant Director for Curatorial Affairs 1983–92. Foremost among current staff members who deserve our praise is Dare Myers Hartwell, who has served as the guiding force behind the restoration of the Salon Doré and the creation of this publication. She led the research, selected the restorers, carried out the treatment of the ceiling mural with her colleagues, and still works to complete the restoration through the acquisition of original furnishings and curtains for the room. Other staff members who deserve special recognition are Susan Badder, Curator of Education; Steven Brown, Operations Manager; Marisa Keller, Curatorial Assistant (1989–93) and now Archivist; Cindy Rom and Kirsten Verdi, Registrars; Rosemary DeRosa, Contract Registrar; Clyde Paton and Greg Angelone, Preparators; and the Corcoran Graphics Department: Lisa Ratkus, Design Director; Nancy Van Meter; and especially the designer of this publication, Tim Connor, Design Assistant. We also thank Alan Abrams for his invaluable help with the color separations and printing, and our capable editor, Nancy Eickel.

From the Clark family, we are grateful for the support of three of the Senator's great-grandsons: André Baeyens, John H. Hall, Jr., and Lewis R. M. Hall. We also thank Rosamond Westmoreland, Catherine Rogers, Elizabeth Parr, Hervé Gehler, and Nancie Ravenel, who, in addition to working as conservators in the Salon Doré, reviewed the account of the restoration for this publication. Michael B. Sassani videotaped the restoration of the ceiling mural, and Matt Dibble and Linda Lewett videotaped the gilding process, providing us with hours of fascinating footage that we hope to edit and expand into a twenty-seven-minute documentary on the history of the room and its restoration.

Dr. Bruno Pons labored earnestly to complete his article on the Salon Doré just before his untimely death in 1995. We are grateful for his expertise and advice as well as the charm, good humor, and generosity of spirit which made knowing him such a pleasure.

Finally, the Corcoran Gallery is indebted to the many donors who so generously supported the restoration of the Salon Doré. Major donors are listed elsewhere, but we particularly want to acknowledge the importance of the funding provided by an anonymous donor, the Morris and Gwendolyn Cafritz Foundation, the Getty Grant Program, the Florence Gould Foundation, and the family of Constance B. Mellon. We also wish to thank the Samuel H. Kress Foundation, an anonymous donor, and Mr. and Mrs. John H. Hall, Jr., for providing funding for this publication.

1   Christian Baulez, "L'hôtel de Clermont: 69, rue de Varenne," in *Le Faubourg Saint-Germain, La rue de Varenne* (Paris: Délégation à l'Action Artistique de la Ville de Paris et Société d'Histoire et d'Archéologie du VII Arrondissement, 1981), p. 72.

2   A popular decorative motif in France, trophies feature an assemblage of objects with a common theme and derive from the ancient Greek practice of hanging captured weapons from a tree or standard on the battlefield.

3   F. Contet, *Les Vieux Hôtels de Paris: Le Faubourg Saint Germain* (Paris, 1911), pp. 3–4, pls. 4 and 5. Christian Baulez, Conservateur en Chef, Musée National des châteaux de Versailles et de Trianon, identified the furniture as belonging to Monsieur and Madame Aubrey-Vitet.

4   Jean-François Méjanès, *Les collections du comte d'Orsay: dessins du Musée du Louvre: LXXVIII exposition du Cabinet des dessins* [The Collections of the Count d'Orsay: drawings from the Louvre museum: LXXVIII exhibition of the drawing collection], (Paris: Ministère de la Culture, Éditions de la Réunion des musées nationaux, 1983), pp. 14, 18–20.

5   According to Jean-Nérée Ronfort, this type of alabaster, which is known by several names in France, including *alabâtre fleuri, alabâtre oriental, alabâtre rubané,* and *alabâtre de Palombara,* probably came originally from an ancient quarry in Asia Minor, near the ruins of the city of Hierapolis in Phrygia (modern-day Pamukkale, Turkey). Stone was not quarried from this site after the Imperial Roman period.
    The pilfering of rare stone from ancient monuments and its reuse in contemporary art and architecture was common in Rome from the Middle Ages through the eighteenth century. Comte d'Orsay's alabaster most closely resembles that found in the ruins of the Gardens Lamiani, named after the family that originally owned it, the Aelii Lamia. The gardens were situated on the Esquiline Hill in what is today the area between the Piazza Vittorio and the Piazza Dante. Emperor Caligula (A.D. 12–41) built a residence here, and parts of the pavement of the gallery of his palace have been reused in the floor of the Palazzo dei Conservatori on the Capitoline Hill. Slabs of alabaster that seem to share a common origin with that of comte d'Orsay's pier tables may be seen here. (Information taken from a memorandum to Dare Myers Hartwell, 16 February 1998.)

6   Lewis Hall, quoting Carl B. Glasscock in the introduction to *The William A. Clark Collection: An exhibition marking the 50th Anniversary of the installation of The Clark Collection at The Corcoran Gallery of Art, Washington, D.C.* (Washington, D.C.: Corcoran Gallery of Art, 1978), p. 2. Other details of Clark's life come from this source.

7   W. A. Clark to Frederick McGuire, in a letter dated 2 March 1909. Director's correspondence file, box 1, folder 36, in the Archives of the Corcoran Gallery and School of Art.

Elévation de la façade et Porte cocher, du côté de la rue, de l'hotel de Clermont rue de Varennes.

Fig. 1ᵉʳᵉ

Elévation des Ailes et Pavillons de la Basse-cour

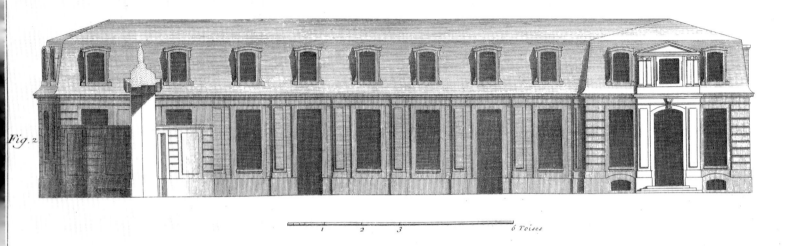

Fig. 2

1   2   3   6 Toises

Elévation de la façade du côté du jardin de l'hotel de Clermont appartenant a Madᵉ. de Sessac rue de Varennes a Paris.

Du dessein du Sʳ. le Blond Architecte

Fig. 2.

Rampe   Rampe

Elévation du côté de la Cour.

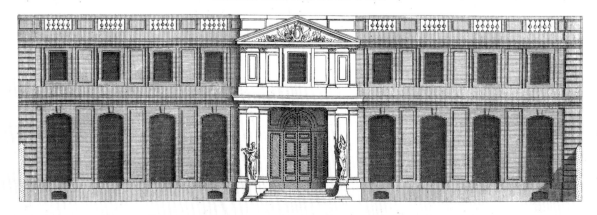

Fig. 1ᵉʳᵉ

1   2   3   4   5   6 Toises

The Hôtel d'Orsay in Paris

BRUNO PONS

A HÔTEL OF THE FAUBOURG SAINT-GERMAIN

In the late eighteenth century, during the reign of Louis XVI, the hôtel d'Orsay[1] was one of the most beautiful private mansions of the faubourg Saint-Germain in Paris. This was not because it was larger than the other hôtels or its architecture more innovative. It was renowned for its interiors, which were frequently redecorated to serve as a backdrop for the comte d'Orsay's important art collections that he constantly enlarged during his lifetime.

The faubourg Saint-Germain was named after the famous abbey of Saint-Germain des Prés. As its name (Saint-Germain in the Fields) indicates, the abbey was erected in the fields outside Paris on the left bank of the Seine and, in the Middle Ages, possessed walls to ensure its own defense. In addition to the area protected by those walls, the abbey and its powerful abbot also controlled a great deal of land. For the most part, this land was planted with vegetable gardens, the produce of which was sold at markets in Paris. Religious and charitable institutions dedicated to saving souls and taking care of the sick and the poor were also established on the abbey's land. As early as the seventeenth century, urbanization of the Seine's left bank in Paris grew irreversibly westward, particularly after the creation of the hôtel des Invalides by Louis XIV in 1671. The king had planned to erect this building for retired soldiers far from the center of Paris, but in the end, the hôtel des Invalides served as a center for urban development. At a time when construction was booming in Paris and members of the aristocracy wished to build vast, beautiful mansions with large gardens, the extensive area between the Luxembourg Palace and the Invalides gradually filled with magnificent residences. Several princes of royal blood, including the duchesse de Bourbon, the prince de Conti, the duchesse du Maine, and the prince de Condé, moved into this new district at the beginning of the 1720s, and its reputation was made. The new area soon became popular and was quickly nicknamed the "noble suburb," for it was the favorite dwelling place of the French high aristocracy.

By contrast, the Marais district on the right bank remained dominated by the parliamentary nobles and magistrates. The faubourg Saint-Honoré was home to financiers and those of the nobility who were close to the financial world, and the northern Parisian boulevards were inhabited by a picturesque mix of bankers, nobles, and provocative actresses. It was in this area of the right bank, and not in the faubourg Saint-Germain, that the bold, new architecture of Etienne-Louis Boullée (1728–1799) and Claude-Nicolas Ledoux (1736–1806), with its luxurious, somewhat ostentatious mansions, was erected around 1770.

Within the faubourg Saint-Germain itself, some areas were more highly prized than others. One was the south side of the rue de Varenne, where the hôtel d'Orsay is located. This furthest southern limit of the faubourg allowed direct access to the country as well as space for gardens that were far larger than those of the other hôtels of the faubourg. Among the famous gardens of the residences neighboring the hôtel d'Orsay are the hôtel Biron (1727–28, now the Musée Rodin) and the hôtel de Broglie (1754, rebuilt in 1782) to the west in the direction of the Invalides; and to the east, the hôtel de La Rochefoucauld (1776), the hôtel d'Estampes (built in 1705 and modified in 1719), the hôtel de Mazarin (1703, 1719, modified in 1736), the hôtel de Matignon (1722), the hôtel de Boisgelin (1732–33), and finally the hôtels de Jaucourt (1777) and d'Havrincourt (1770). These neighboring gardens sometimes included small pavilions and often offered views from one garden to the next. Such amenities made this part of Paris unique.

The Comte d'Orsay and the Hôtel d'Orsay

In 1768, Pierre-Gaspard-Marie Grimod, comte d'Orsay, purchased the hôtel de Clermont, which had been built in 1708 for the marquise de Saissac (née Jeanne-Thérèse-Pélagie d'Albert de Luynes) and was located in one of the most desirable areas of the faubourg Saint-Germain, on the south side of the rue de Varenne (figs. 3, 4).[2] For more than sixty years the building had belonged to different branches of the marquise's family, and in the mid-eighteenth century had housed the famous curio cabinets of the duc de Chaulnes, an amateur scientist.

The comte d'Orsay (fig. 5) was the posthumous son of the enormously wealthy financier Pierre Grimod Dufort (1692–1748), a *fermier général* (tax collector for the king) and an administrator of the post office, and his third wife, the noblewoman Marie-Antoinette de Caulaincourt. The count's origins destined him for the right bank (where his father had sumptuously renovated the hôtel Chamillart), and as a young child he

and his mother lived on the aristocratic Place Vendôme in the faubourg Saint-Honoré.[3] Eventually, however, his noble mother decided to break with his father's family and the financial district, and they crossed the Seine to the left bank, where they rented the hôtel de Châteauneuf on the quai Malaquais from the rash Nicolas Duvaucel, seigneur de la Norville.

Having lived with his mother in a different milieu from that of his bourgeois father, the young man was quite self-conscious about his origins. In purchasing the hôtel de Clermont, the comte d'Orsay was no longer in the world of financiers but among the highest members of the aristocracy. From his father he inherited a taste for both luxury and the fine arts as well as a flair for profitable alliances. His contemporaries all agreed: the count's ambition was impossible to hide. Sébastien-Roch-Nicholas Chamfort mocked the young man who was "known for his mania to be a man of quality" but whose manners were sometimes quite ridiculous.[4] Louis Petit de Bachaumont had no trouble discovering Orsay's secret: "Being ashamed of his birth, which did not correspond to his ambitions, he tried to cover it up by marrying women whose rank in society was infinitely superior to his."[5] This was also the impression Orsay produced on his future father-in-law, the maréchal duc de Croÿ, who was rather displeased with his daughter's marriage to the count on 31 December 1770. Nevertheless, Orsay was seductive and succeeded beyond all expectations.

The comte d'Orsay was only nineteen years old when he purchased the hôtel de Clermont. One of his first modifications was to remodel an apartment for the future comtesse d'Orsay, Marie-Louise-Albertine, princesse de Croÿ-Molembais (fig. 6). Later trips to Italy and the growing size of his art collection called for further renovations of his home, which were carried out without altering the earlier modifications.[6] Orsay's ambitions demanded that he continually aggrandize his house. After the countess died in childbirth in 1772, Orsay traveled in Italy from 1775 to 1778, and his taste for the fine arts grew stronger, as did his preference for cosmopolitan society. His first concern was to remarry: "He presented himself to twenty great families in Europe experiencing stiff rejections until the Prince de Bartenstein, favorably impressed with the magnificence of M[onsieur] d'Orsay, gave him one of his daughters in marriage."[7] The prince's enthusiasm

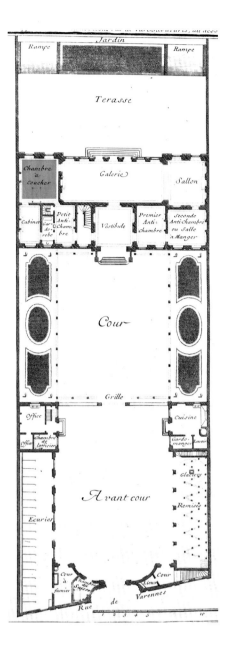

FIGURE 7

Hôtel de Clermont, original plan by the building's architect, Jean-Baptiste-Alexandre Le Blond. The location of the Salon Doré is marked chambre à coucher *because it was originally the bedroom of the marquise de Saissac. Published by Jacques-François Blondel in* Architecture françoise *(1752). The American Institute of Architects Library and Archives, Washington, D.C.*

was perhaps due to the renovation of Orsay's Paris hôtel. Undertaken by several architects beginning in 1781, it was designed to enhance the display of scores of sculptures and art objects that the count had gathered, more or less with discernment, in Italy and France. The count, however, would have to wait until 1784 for his marriage with the daughter of the ruling prince of Hohenlohe-Waldenbourg to take place.

The Salon of the Comtesse d'Orsay: Architecture

The contractor Pierre Convers was at work on the hôtel by late 1769. The marquise de Saissac's former bedroom became the Salon Doré (fig. 7).[8] Its renovation, commissioned in 1770, was completed just in time for the count's wedding, which surprised everyone, to the princesse de Croÿ-Molembais in late December 1770. The Salon Doré, part of the comtesse d'Orsay's suite of rooms on the ground floor, overlooked the garden and was used as a room for entertaining guests (fig. 13). The count reserved the second floor for himself, but for his wife he wanted an amazing decor worthy of a true princess.

Occasioned as it was by the count's wedding, the decor of the Salon Doré celebrated the union of marital love and military virtue, or perhaps more appropriately in the count's case, the celebration of glory brought forth by conquest. While vain, Orsay was still too young to have formed an original personal taste. Disliking affectation and fearing innovation, he demanded a noble and classical style for his house.

The original disposition of the decorative elements in the Salon Doré in the eighteenth century (when it was still in Paris) is worthy of study. The salon was nearly square and contained Corinthian pilasters (that is to say, the highest and most elaborate architectural order) that framed gilded trophies set on panels. Its design owes its originality to the enormous mirrors, made of four sections of glass, which alternate with the pilasters and are set in frames with rectangular corners rather than round arches.[9]

Naturally, the dimensions of the room and its general arrangement dated back to the construction of the original building in 1708. Located at the eastern end of the apartments, this room was the last one of the great apartment and gave access to the small apartments beyond. It opened onto the terrace and the garden of the mansion through two French windows. A slightly narrower wall mirror was placed between these two windows (fig. 9). The arrangement of this wall with its ternary rhythm established the pattern for the new decor prepared for the comtesse d'Orsay. The ensemble formed by the two French windows and the wall mirror was repeated on the opposite wall in the form of three large wall mirrors, whose rectangular corners repeated the shape of the windows (fig. 10). This unusual decor was no doubt costly. In the middle of the two remaining walls, two more wall mirrors of the same design were installed to face each other, in keeping with the rules of contemporary French decoration: one was placed above the fireplace and the second opposite it (figs. 11, 12). The unity of the room was thus created by an ensemble of similarly shaped wall mirrors and windows that constituted the true architecture of the salon. At the same time the Corinthian pilasters, the four trophy panels, and the rich cornice gave the room a noble, if not antique, character.

Garlands of rosebuds (the flowers of love) mixed with meadow flowers (symbols of marriage) were displayed everywhere and lent a festive air that prevented any hint of severity. The garlands extended across the mirrors and either were fixed to the edges by interlacing ribbons or were held above the doors by lively cupids, as in *Le coucher de la mariée* (The Bride's Bedtime), a gouache by Pierre-Antoine Bandouin engraved by Jean-

FIGURE 8

Jean-Michel Moreau, etching after Pierre-Antoine Baudouin,
Le coucher de la mariée, 47 × 33.9 cm (18 ½ × 13⅜
in.), National Gallery of Art, Widener Collection,
Washington, D.C.

Michel Moreau the younger that dates exactly to the same time as the salon of the comtesse d'Orsay (fig. 8).[10] Love also forms the theme of the antique-style medallions above the doors, where vestal virgins tend the flame of love or make sacrifices to it. Garlands similar to those on the mirrors also adorned four corner tables (*encoignures*) (pl. 5) and two console tables.[11] Such elements of furniture were considered part of the architectural decoration, and presumably the chairs placed against the walls also echoed some of the motifs of the decor. The garland motif was already present on the door of the hôtel that opened onto the rue de Varenne.

No doubt some influence of the Greek style can also be seen here. The Greek style introduced heavy, thick garlands of laurel leaves in unexpected places, as in the desk at the château de Chantilly (ca. 1756–57) created for Ange-Laurent Lalive de Jully, a wealthy collector who helped introduce the *goût Grec*. Garlands descending from a crown of flowers at the top of the mirrors in the comtesse d'Orsay's salon recall that style, but at the same time they differ in their execution, for they seem to be visibly added on top of the architectural decoration. No longer restricted to being an ornamental element, garlands became a fairly popular, independent motif in the 1770s, when they were used as an additional mark of wealth.

Such garlands could also be found on the columns of the rotunda of Vauxhall. Built by the architect L. D. Le Camus in 1771, the interior decor of Vauxhall is today known through drawings made by Gabriel de Saint-Aubin in 1772 (Wallace Collection).[12] In a more natural style, garlands twisted around pilasters and columns in the decoration of

FIGURE 9

Hôtel de Clermont, Salon Doré, present-day view of the window wall with plaster casts of the original paneling. In the eighteenth century a mirror instead of a trophy panel would have been placed between the windows. The room is now used as an office area.

FIGURE 10

Hôtel de Clermont, Salon Doré, present-day view of the mirror wall with plaster casts of the original paneling.

FIGURE 11

Hôtel de Clermont, Salon Doré, present-day view of the mantel wall with plaster casts of the original paneling. According to Bruno Pons, the red marble mantel is probably not original.

FIGURE 12

Hôtel de Clermont, Salon Doré, present-day view of the wall opposite the mantel with plaster casts of the original paneling.

FIGURE 13

Hôtel de Clermont, present-day view from the garden. The Salon Doré's two rectangular French windows are on the ground floor at the right. The comte d'Orsay's monogram appears in the ironwork on the second-story balcony (see below).

the pavilion called *joli colifichet* (pretty trinket) that was erected for the duchesse de Bourbon in the gardens of the Palais Bourbon (1772–75). There again, garlands gave the illusion of having been a later addition, as if included for a celebration in the garden pavilion, just as garlands set the theme of the perpetual wedding celebration in the comtesse d'Orsay's Salon Doré.[13]

The two side walls of the salon (the fireplace wall and the one opposite it) varied the decorative scheme. In addition to the tall Corinthian pilasters and the narrow panels decorated at the top with garlands, four great carved and gilded trophy panels symbolize Love, Victory, Music, and the Arts and Sciences, and somewhat recall the famous gilded bronze trophies by the goldsmith Pierre Ladoireau (1676–1711) in the Hall of Mirrors at Versailles, which had remained a model for French architects (pls. 28, 30, 33, cover). In addition, two double doors divided each wall. The count did not commission paintings to decorate the space above the doors because at that time fashion demanded that the art of painting should no longer be confined to such secondary locations. Paintings were installed elsewhere, and their place above the doors was given over to sculpture.

It is now known that the salon of the hôtel d'Orsay was one of the first decorative works of the great architect Jean-François-Thérèse Chalgrin (1734–1811). A pupil of Etienne-Louis Boullée, Chalgrin had returned from Rome in 1763 and would become architect for the comte de Provence (brother of Louis XVI) in 1774.

In 1771, Chalgrin made a payment to the sculptor Elie Janel, whose workshop was located on the rue de Bourgogne. This suggests that Janel may have carved part of the

FIGURE 14

Attributed to Henri Piètre, a drawing for a salon in the hôtel Mélusine, 1765. Service Photographique des Archives Nationales, Paris.

paneling of the Salon Doré. More certainly, the sculpture in the four spaces above the doors is the work of the sculptor François-Joseph Duret (1729–1816), Chalgrin's frequent collaborator.[14] Since Duret had sculpted the figures of the torchbearers in the Hall of Mirrors at Versailles the previous year, he seemed an appropriate choice to sculpt the playful putti above the doors. It was a familiar theme for Duret, who delivered his work in 1770. The putti are similar to those he had just executed for two other decorative projects headed by Chalgrin: the hôtel of the comte de Saint-Florentin, minister of the king, on the place Louis XV, and that of the prominent actress Mademoiselle Luzy on the rue Férou.[15] The price of eight hundred livres asked by Duret for the hôtel d'Orsay work is significantly higher than the price charged for the work in the other two hôtels because the figures were carved out of wood rather than cast in plaster.

The flower paintings that decorate the door panels remain a problem. Since the panels of the "replica" salon in Paris are copies, the doors now in Washington were certainly part of the original room in the hôtel de Clermont.[16] They could have been added at a later date, however, perhaps during the modifications carried out in the hôtel in the nineteenth century. It is difficult to critique these flower decorations. The quality of the original panels is rather poor, probably because they were frequently repainted and the restorations were more or less faithful to the original, and in addition, I do not really know of any comparable decorations. Some drawings dating to 1765 and attributed to the architect Henri Piètre (ca. 1725–ca. 1785) for a salon in the hôtel Mélusine (which is, in fact, an annex of the Palais-Royal of the ducs d'Orléans) show door panels painted with bouquets of cut flowers that are represented in a naturalistic fashion quite similar to those of the Salon Doré (fig. 14).[17] At the same time, some large bouquets of painted flowers were also part of a famous project included in the series of decorations prepared in 1766 by the architect Victor Louis (1731–1807) in Paris for the royal palace in Warsaw.[18]

Finally, in 1771–72, the painter and decorator Pierre-Hyacinthe Deleuze, who had worked with Chalgrin several times, painted a thousand little bouquets of "colored flowers" in the study of the prince de Condé at the Palais Bourbon.[19] The visual intent in the study was to imitate in painting the Sèvres porcelain plaques that were produced and sold to decorate small rooms and particularly furniture like that made by Martin Carlin (ca. 1730–1785).[20] All these decorations have disappeared, proving their fragility. Was the comtesse d'Orsay's salon one of the last creations to bear witness to this fashion?

Executed at a time when painted ceilings were in fashion, the ceiling of the salon was decorated with *L'Apothéose de Psyché* (The Apotheosis of Psyche, fig. 15), a large composition on canvas by Hugues Taraval (1729–1785). A sketch of this oft-told fable of impetuous love was presented by the artist at the Salon of 1773, but the execution of the ceiling painting seems to precede that date.[21] Very little of Taraval's decorative work remains except for the ceilings of the hôtel d'Orsay. Unfortunately, the original ceiling of the salon of the comtesse d'Orsay did not follow the paneling to the United States. It was separated from the rest of the decoration and moved to the hôtel Veil-Picard on the boulevard de Courcelles, where it was eventually destroyed during the demolition of that building in 1970.

The ceiling painted on canvas (pl. 22) by Taraval for the adjacent dining room of the hôtel d'Orsay was moved to New York. Simpler than the original salon painting, it depicts a sky filled with flying putti. Medallions at the center of each border are held by groups of two women painted in grisaille to imitate sculpture. These figures represent the Four Seasons, Painting, Sculpture, Music, and Poetry.[22] In the 1770s, when the size of the room allowed it, sculpture groups in stucco frequently decorated salons and were most often placed in the middle of each side, above the cornice, where they clearly emerged from coves. Ceiling painters imitated that style, especially in rooms with relatively low ceilings, such as those found in the hôtel d'Orsay.

The Furnishings of the Salon of the Comtesse d'Orsay

The comte d'Orsay's unexpected marriage to the princesse de Croÿ-Molembais would have been beneficial if it had lasted longer, but the countess soon died in childbirth. According to the marquis de Bombelles: "M. d'Orsay, who could not bear the thought of having been born in a bourgeois family, first married a daughter of the illustrious house of Croÿ. More fortunate than he should have been in such a disproportionate alliance, he found in his wife a charming companion, an excellent domestic manager and, had she lived, she might have made of her husband a reasonable man."[23] The count commissioned the distinguished sculptor Claude-Michel Clodion to execute the mausoleum he built for his wife in the parish church in Orsay.

The household inventory drawn up in February 1774 provides an idea of the sumptuous character of the comtesse d'Orsay's Salon Doré.[24]

Inventory drawn up after the death of Marie Louise Albertine Amélie de Croÿ-Molembais, comtesse d'Orsay

In the salon located at the left of the dining room and overlooking the garden

Item *two andirons, shovel, tongs and pincers in polished iron with ornaments and gilded military trophies, four gilded three-branched sconces estimated together at four thousand* livres, *these* . . . . . . 4,000 L.

Item *a gilded clock executed in Paris by Caffiery [sic] set in a globe supported by a dragon, indicating the hours, the minutes and the lunar calendar estimated at three thousand* livres, *this* . . . . . . 3,000 L.

Item *two console tables of wood gilded in different colors of gold with tops of veined alabaster surrounded by a strip of gilded copper, four matching corner tables, two thousand* livres, *these* . . . . . . 2,000 L.

Item *a rolltop desk in satinwood decorated with flowers and musical instruments including three drawers with gilded ornaments, a double sided desk made of redwood with gilded copper candle-rings, a small writing table in rosewood estimated at six hundred* livres, *these* . . . . . . 600 L.

Item *a bunch of artificial wax flowers in their French porcelain bowl, a mantel garniture of two alabaster and three agate vases estimated at six hundred* livres, *these* . . . . . . 600 L.

Item *four large armchairs* (bergères) *in gilded wood upholstered in* dauphine *fabric of colored flowers on a crimson background stuffed with horse hair estimated at three hundred* livres, *these......*300 L.

Item *a card table covered in green fabric estimated at fifteen* livres, *this......*15 L.

Item *a three-seat sofa in carved wood gilded in different colors of gold and eight matching arm-chairs* (fauteuils) *all upholstered with crimson and flowered Gobelins tapestry stuffed with horse hair, two feather sofa pillows upholstered with the same tapestry, six plain gilded wood armchairs* (fauteuils) *stuffed with horse hair and upholstered with petit point tapestry with their feather pillows covered with the same tapestry and eight flat-back chairs* (chaises à la reine) *all similar and estimated together at four thousand* livres, *these......*4,000 L.

*Regarding a mantelpiece and five wall mirrors including one placed between two windows, no estimate was done because those elements are embedded in the paneling and will perpetually remain there, that is why we only mention them in our account, therefore......*NO VALUATION.

Plus a screen made of Gobelins tapestry with crimson background and flowers similar to that of the aforementioned furniture on a gilded wooden frame, two window curtains made of four pieces of crimson damask, measuring each three lez by four aulnes with a descent of similar damask, the whole being adorned with a band of imitation gold and estimated together at eight hundred livres, *these......*800 L.

The mere reading of the document suggests that, ultimately, the architectural decoration was not the richest element of the salon. Yet, without the vital identifications of some of the existing furniture provided by Christian Baulez, we would still be ignorant of the extent of the room's wealth.

The rolltop desk in the salon of the countess has not been located, but it is known that the comte d'Orsay owned another rolltop desk, one of the most famous pieces made by cabinetmaker Jean-Henri Riesener (1734–1806; fig. 16). That desk, today in the Wallace Collection in London, was once thought to have belonged to the king of Poland.[25] In fact, the comte d'Orsay commissioned the piece for himself. It is a slightly simplified replica of the desk begun by Jean-François Oeben (ca. 1720–1763), completed by Riesener and installed in Louis XV's interior study at Versailles in 1769. A masterpiece of bronze and inlay technique, the desk bears the count's monograms of *OR* and *ORS* (a play on his name). Like the desk made for the king, this desk is decorated with trophies of the Sciences and the Arts, and of Love and War. This last theme of Love and War was flattering to the count—although he was only a *capitaine des dragons* in the Lorraine-Bauffremont regiment, and in truth, it was more appropriate for the illustrious house of Croÿ—and he had it repeated on the trophy panels and the fireplace tools of the Salon Doré. Clearly, Orsay liked to display his monogram. His desk is a proof of it: even the key still bears the monogram *ORS.* His monogram also marks the drawings in his collection, the railings of the balconies overlooking the garden (fig. 13), and a beautiful plan of the

hôtel. The count's arrogance was such that he even modified the sign of the Roman legions carved on the trophy of Victory in the Salon Doré, substituting the traditional S.P.Q.R. (*Senatus Populusque Romanus*—the Senate and the People of Rome) with a strange SPORQ, which is more Orsay than Roman (pl. 1).

The clock with a dragon by the sculptor and bronze caster Jacques Caffieri (b. 1725) came from Grimod Dufort, the count's father. On the four corner tables whose tops were executed not in marble but in the more valuable alabaster, the count soon installed bronze groups of the four seasons—*Zéphyr et Flore, Le chariot de Cérès, Bacchus et Ariane,* and *Vénus et Vulcain*—purchased for 4,800 livres at the auction of the Gaignat collection in 1769.[26] At Orsay's request, these figures were set on bronze pedestals and mounted as five-branched candelabra by Phillipe Caffieri (1714–1774; pl. 5).[27]

The salon's furnishings allowed the eye to linger on the garniture of the mantelpiece, the alabaster and agate vases, and a bowl made of Sèvres porcelain. And one could admire and enjoy the chairs and the large three-person sofa whose wooden frames, possibly the work of Louis Delanois (1731–1792), were upholstered with Gobelins tapestries woven with bouquets of flowers on a red background. These chairs were possibly similar to those executed for the château de La Roche Guyon at about the same time.[28]

Can a more precise picture of the arrangement of the furniture in the salon be drawn from the inventory? The sconces can be easily located: one on each side of the mirror above the fireplace, and one on each side of the wall mirror opposite it. The placement of the garniture of precious vases on the mantelpiece is also indicated in the inventory.

The architectural furniture, to use the eighteenth-century term, comprised the chairs and console tables placed against the wall. Such pieces were considered part of the decorative paneling and were specifically designed and executed for that purpose. In addition to the four corner consoles, whose carved ornaments repeated those of the wall

mirrors, the room included two rectangular consoles, each approximately 1.3 meters wide (51 3/16 inches). These two tables could have been placed symmetrically under the two end mirrors on the wall opposite the windows, flanking the sofa that could have been placed under the middle mirror. Another solution would be to place one table opposite the fireplace and a second between the two windows or under the middle wall mirror, where it would face the windows. These console tables determine the placement of the sofa and the eight armchairs upholstered in Gobelins tapestry, all of which were intended to remain against the walls as a part of the decorative paneling and never used. As mentioned, the sofa could have been placed either facing the fireplace or in the center of the wall opposite the windows. The eight matching armchairs (fauteuils), sometimes grouped by twos, must have been distributed harmoniously around the room, thus reinforcing the visual rhythm of eight pilasters. The red background of their Gobelins tapestry upholstery would have matched the great curtains of crimson damask and given the salon its dominant colors of crimson and gold, colors that were used for the decoration of the royal apartments.

The seats that were meant for use—six armchairs (fauteuils) and eight flat-back chairs (chaises à la reine)—were arranged in the middle of the room. Simpler in design, their wooden frames were uncarved, but as a sign of wealth, they were gilded. Four upholstered armchairs (bergères) would have been placed near the card table. More difficult to determine are the placement of the clock (on a console rather than on the mantelpiece) and the rolltop desk.

As imagined today, the salon seems to have been a great showplace where objects of luxury were gathered and displayed, almost like a collector's cabinet. Yet the bronze sculpture groups that could have been considered art objects were mounted into candelabra and thus transformed into part of the furnishings. Such decoration marked the beginning of an ostentatious luxury that characterized interior decoration in the early years of the reign of Louis XVI. Not only did the decorative seating around the perimeter of the room take on a vital importance but the movable, functional seats were also made more significant by gilding. Like all drawing rooms, the salon, located near the small apartment of the countess, was probably used to play music and games. That would explain the inventory's mention of a card table and four large armchairs, as if suggesting a last game.

Although famous for its riches, the hôtel d'Orsay was not readily accessible. Luc-Vincent Thiéry wrote in his *Guide* of 1787: "M. le comte d'Orsay gathered his collection for his own pleasure and only he and his friends can enjoy it."[29] The statement in the *Guide* was probably used against Orsay during the Revolution, because his manager Vernier insisted otherwise. "This collection, or rather these collections, were so to speak available to the public since all the curious and artists could come and see them in the apartments or the gardens where they were displayed, and even draw after them at any time and at no cost."[30] In fact, the count was leaving France for Germany when the *Guide* was published, and in 1788 he rented his hôtel to William Beckford, a great English collector who was then visiting Paris.

Orsay most assuredly opened the hôtel more liberally to artists. The American painter John Trumbull visited it on 7 August 1786, just before he visited the Invalides.

Tuesday, August 7th. Went to the house of the Count D'orsay, said to be one of the most superb in Paris; it is in truth overloaded with elegance; the furniture is expensive and rich, to a fault; the eye can find no rest; the windows, in one of the apartments looking upon the garden, are of plate glass, only two pieces in each. The picture room contains the most beautiful collection of perfect little things that I have ever seen together; the Visitation of the Virgin, by Rubens- the taking down from the Cross, by Rembrandt- an Infant Saviour, by Vandyck- are superb. Teniers, Paul Potter, Wouvermans, Mieris, Metzu, Netscher, Van Oort, &c. &c., have precious specimens here. Small bronze copies of the finest antique statues, the choicest porcelain, &c. &c. literally crowd every apartment. The dining room is magnificent, ornamented with marble copies of some of the best antiques; the columns which separate the windows are of green and white marble; the windows are of plate glass, of prodigious size; but in my opinion, this room has one inexcusable fault - it looks upon the court yard, where is all the dirty business of the stables, &c., objects far from pleasing to contemplate, in convivial hours. [31]

Regrettably, Orsay's collection did not survive the Revolution.[32] The hôtel was seized and assigned to various administrative commissions before it became the *Lombard des arts* (a pawnshop for artists' deposits), where the dealer Jean-Baptiste Lebrun, husband to the painter Marie-Louise-Elisabeth Vigée-Lebrun, organized auctions and exhibitions. Some painters, including Jacques-Louis David, Joseph-Marie Vien, and Anne-Louis Girodet, were allowed to show their work there, and some architects enjoyed the same privilege. Chalgrin appears on the list of accredited artists, along with Pierre-Adrien Pâris, Etienne-Louis Boullée, and one of the brothers Peyre.

Finally, it served as headquarters to the *société des jeux gymniques* (Society of Gymnastic Games), which promoted the exercise of body and mind. A brochure on the gymnastic games includes a description of the hôtel d'Orsay in 1797. "The gymnastic games are opening on the rue de Varenne, no. 667, in a house where the most beautiful artistic productions were once gathered, and collectors and the curious used to meet. The house still contains beauties inherent to the place...."[33] The Salon Doré is described as being the sixth room.

Crossing again the previous room, one reaches a vast salon. It is decorated in the Corinthian order with its cornice gilded in different golds. There are four great trophies dedicated to love, victory, music and the sciences and arts. These attributes of the gymnastic games [sic] are located between the pilasters; the remaining intervals are occupied by mirrors as high as the ceiling. A beautifully executed railing crowns the architecture and serves as a frame for the ceiling painting representing Cupid accompanied by the Pleasures leading Psyche to Olympus, where a gathering of gods can be seen. The subject is treated in a pleasant fashion and honors Taraval's talent. [34]

This institution did not last very long, for it had to compete with other societies whose locations were better suited to such pleasures than at the far end of the faubourg Saint-Germain.

The Salon Doré in the Nineteenth and Twentieth Centuries

In 1838, the hôtel was acquired by the comtesse Duchâtel, wife of Louis-Philippe's minister.[35] By that time it was once again well appointed by a family who appreciated the arts and possessed significant paintings and beautiful eighteenth-century furniture, including some pieces that were later bequeathed to the Louvre. From 1869 to 1880, the family hired the services of Emile Peyre, a dealer and decorator with offices at 35, rue Saint-Georges "to supervise the renovation of the hôtel de Paris, either to guide it or to acquire the necessary decorative objects or curiosities."[36] At the time of her death in 1878, the comtesse Duchâtel was survived by a son who served as a diplomat in Denmark. Her daughter married the duc de La Trémoille, who lived in the hôtel after his marriage in 1862. He moved to the avenue Gabriel in 1880 after he tried to purchase the hôtel de l'Impératrice on the rue de l'Elysée. Emile Peyre was put in charge of decorating his new house.[37]

The circumstances of the transfer of the salon to the United States are still not precisely known, but it is certain that the removal took place before the Duchâtel heirs sold the hôtel to Eugène Aubry-Vitet in 1905.[38] Possibly it could have occurred in the late nineteenth century, when the hôtel was threatened with demolition.

Senator William Andrews Clark (1839–1925) reconstructed the salon in his amazing New York "palace" located at Fifth Avenue and Seventy-seventh Street (fig. 19). Designed in 1895 by the French architect Henri Deglane (1855–1931), the mansion was erected to house Clark's art collection. While it included several stylized period salons—a Renaissance room, a Louis XV salon, and the great Louis XVI Salon Doré—only the latter contained authentic elements. Instead of a square salon in the French manner, the reconstruction of the Salon Doré in New York altered the shape into a rectangular room or gallery, corresponding more to the Anglo-Saxon idea of an exhibition hall for paintings and art objects. Clark lived in his mansion until his death.

The hôtel on the rue de Varenne was not left entirely bare of its decoration after the removal of the salon: a copy was executed and left in its place. In theory, the salon became a double room, with the original room in New York and the copy reconstructed on the rue de Varenne. The reality is far less simple.

"Replacement by a copy" was a clause sometimes included in the sales of great pieces of architecture at the end of the nineteenth century. Generally, however, those copies were extremely simplified. Since this was not the case for the hôtel d'Orsay, several questions arise: Why was the decoration sold? Why were difficult removals, such as that of the ceilings, undertaken? Why was an expensive reconstruction made in a hôtel still inhabited by a well-to-do family, and is it possible that the copy was initially intended to be sold? At this time the fashion for reproduction paneling stimulated the execution of high-quality copies, and the great interiors dismantled by decorators were all copied, used for casts, and, one could say, repeated in several editions.

In fact, it appears that part of the original decoration remained in place on the rue de Varenne, complemented by copies of pieces now in the Unites States and vice versa. Proof of this is found in the accounts of the sculptor Duret, which indicate that the sculptures above the doors were carved in wood. The four decorations above the doors currently in place on the rue de Varenne are indeed carved in wood, while the decorations at the Corcoran are plaster casts. In contrast, the trophy panels on the rue de Varenne follow two models, Love and Victory, repeated three times for one and two times for the other. Four of the trophy panels occupy their original positions in the room while the fifth, a reproduction of Love, has been placed between the two French windows in the space once occupied by a wall mirror at the time of the comte d'Orsay. Such a repetition of themes in the same locale is foreign to eighteenth-century conceptions. At the

Corcoran, however, six trophies with different themes are in place: the four ancient ones of Love, Victory, Music, and the Arts and Sciences surely came from the hôtel d'Orsay, but two "modern" trophies in the eighteenth-century genre were commissioned by Senator Clark as part of the enlargement of his salon. These trophies represent modern subjects: sports with, among other things, a snowshoe (a frank reference to the modern world), and music and French classical theater, an evocation of the heritage of the ancient world (pls. 31, 32).

The Artists of the Salon Doré: Jean-François-Thérèse Chalgrin

The salon of the hôtel d'Orsay was one of the first decorative works of the great architect Jean-François-Thérèse Chalgrin. Trained in the studio of Jean-Nicolas Servandoni (1695–1766), Chalgrin later became a student of Etienne-Louis Boullée. He won the grand prize of the Académie in 1758 with his submission of a modest but truly original project that suggests the distinctive style that would define his career. Shortly afterwards Chalgrin went to Rome, where he remained until 1763. Upon his return to France, he worked with the architect Moreau-Desproux for the city of Paris, where his work was noticed by Henri-Léonard Bertin and the comte de Saint-Florentin, both ministers in charge of the city. Chalgrin was employed by both these men as early as 1767, before he built and decorated the hôtel de Langeac for the mistress of the comte de Saint-Florentin. (Thomas Jefferson rented this hôtel during his ambassadorship in Paris.) Thanks to the support of the comte de Saint-Florentin, Chalgrin was commissioned to draw up plans for the church of Saint-Philippe du Roule, probably as early as 1768 and possibly even in 1765, although construction did not begin until 1774. This building received favorable atten-

Sur nom d'architecte des Monsieur
Ce 16 mars 1781 Chalgrin

FIGURE 18

Jean-François-Thérèse Chalgrin, design for a salon de compagnie, 1781. Musée des arts décoratifs, Paris.

tion because of its basilical plan (an innovation in French architecture) and its beautiful and simple classical style. At the same time, Chalgrin was commissioned to rebuild the church of the seminary of the Saint-Esprit (1768), and he provided the design for the room in which the comte de Mercy-Argenteau, ambassador of Empress Marie-Thérèse, held a ball in his Paris residence at the Petit-Luxembourg in honor of the marriage of the dauphin and Marie-Antoinette in 1770 (fig. 17). With that, Chalgrin's reputation was established.

His success was such that he came to work for the two brothers of King Louis XVI, the comte de Provence (the future Louis XVIII) and the comte d'Artois (the future Charles X). Chalgrin served the comte d'Artois as a manager from 1777 to 1779, a position he no doubt obtained through Boullée. When the residence of the comte de Provence was being built, Chalgrin became his head architect, working mainly at the château de Brunoy, at the Palais du Luxembourg, and in the count's pavilion in Versailles. He submitted a project for the construction of stables for the comtesse d'Artois in the city of Versailles before he erected the pavilion and the gardens of the comtesse de Provence in Montreuil, near Versailles. His duties as head architect for the king's brother became his main activity, but he was also asked to complete the towers of the church of Saint-Sulpice. Soon known as one of the busiest architects in Paris who was not employed in the service of the king, Chalgrin's reputation attracted numerous young foreign students who sought his training. This aspect of Chalgrin's activity is still little known.

Around 1769–70, when the comte d'Orsay selected his architect, Chalgrin was beginning to be known in the field of private architecture through his work for Bertin at the

hôtel de Saint-Florentin in Chatou, near Paris, and at the hôtel of Mademoiselle Luzy. Although he was subsequently better known for his public architecture, Chalgrin continued his activity in the area of decoration, submitting a design for a table to the duchesse de Mazarin in 1781; she, however, chose a design by François-Joseph Bélanger (now in the Frick Collection, New York).[39] A drawing for a window wall for a salon by Chalgrin, signed and dated 1781, is in the Musée des arts décoratifs (fig. 18). Lastly, Chalgrin participated in the decoration of the tribune of the organ of Saint-Sulpice and in the works commissioned by the comte de Provence.

After the French Revolution, Chalgrin resumed renovating the Palais du Luxembourg. He was no longer employed by the comte de Provence, however, but by the Directoire (the governing body of France from 1795 to 1799). He was also honored with a commission for the plan of the Arc de Triomphe (1806–11) before he died.

Hugues Taraval

The son of Guillaume Taraval (1701–1750), painter to King Fredrik I of Sweden, Hugues Taraval returned to Paris after the death of his father. In 1756, he won a grand prize for painting, after which he studied with Carle Van Loo for three years (1756–59) at the Ecole des élèves protégés.[40] Taraval then attended the Académie de France in Rome (1759–63), where Charles-Joseph Natoire, his supervisor, noticed his talent for decorative painting. Indeed, Taraval had already completed one painting before his stay in Rome: *Vierge protégeant les enfants bleus,* which was hanging in the boys' classroom at the hôpital du Saint-Esprit, near the hôtel de Ville.

While still producing easel paintings and regularly exhibiting his work in the Salon from 1765 until his death (except for the Salon of 1771), Taraval won a reputation as a skilled decorative painter. *Le Triomphe de Bacchus* (The Triumph of Bacchus), the decorative work he submitted to the Académie royale de peinture (Royal Academy of Painting) for exhibition in the Salon of 1769, was executed for one of the compartments of the ceiling of the galerie d'Apollon in the Louvre. The commission of the ceiling of the theater room in Mademoiselle Guimard's hôtel, built by Claude-Nicolas Ledoux in the Chaussée d'Antin (1770–72), also brought him attention. He then illustrated *Le Mariage de Saint Louis* (The Wedding of Saint Louis) in 1773, one of the great paintings in the series for the chapel of the Ecole militaire, and completed a painting of the Assumption for the altar of the chapel of the Virgin in the church of Saint-Louis. He was commissioned to paint *Le Triomphe d'Amphitrite* (The Triumph of Amphitrite) in 1777, for a series of *Triomphe des dieux* (Triumph of the gods), which was to be woven at the Manufacture des Gobelins. Here he perpetuated Boucher's style (pl. 6). In 1781, Taraval also executed decorations to be placed above the doors in Marie-Antoinette's apartments in Versailles and at Marly (Wallace Collection) as well as two oval paintings for the chapel of Fontainebleau.

The collaboration between Chalgrin and Taraval (both of whom resided at the Académie de France in Rome at the same time) was not limited to the hôtel d'Orsay. When Chalgrin was in charge of the reconstruction of the Collège royal (Collège de France), he entrusted Taraval with a great portion of the ceiling (ca. 1773–77) representing *La Gloire des princes* (The Princes' Glory; now destroyed). Finally, Taraval's brother, the engraver Louis-Guillaume Taraval, engraved drawings of some of Chalgrin's work. At the hôtel d'Orsay, Hugues Taraval not only worked on the ceilings and part of the furnishings of this room, but he also executed a painted decor of interlacing motifs in the boudoir of the small apartment of the comtesse d'Orsay.

Translated by Chantal Combes and Dare Myers Hartwell

1. The hôtel d'Orsay was known by this name during the tenure of the comte d'Orsay. It is now known as the hôtel de Clermont after its original owner. See the Introduction of this publication for further explanation.

2. For more information see M. Lecomte, *Le Prince des Dandys, le chevalier d'Orsay* (Paris, 1928); M. Dumolin, "L'hôtel Aubry-Vitet," *Bulletin de la Société d'histoire et d'archéologie des VII et XV arrondissements*, no. 30 (Paris, 1928), pp. 160–69; F. Boyer, "Les hôtels parisiens et le château des Grimod d'Orsay au XVIII siècle," *Bulletin de la Société de l'histoire de l'art français* (1951); M. Le Moël, *L'hôtel de Clermont* (Paris, 1978); and J. Wilhelm, "Deux plafonds peints par Hugues Taraval à l'hôtel Grimod d'Orsay," *Bulletin de la Société de l'histoire de l'art français* (1974), pp. 123–30. Christian Baulez brought new insights into the study of the hôtel in the catalogue of the exhibition *Le faubourg Saint-Germain, La rue de Varenne* (Paris: Délégation à 'l Action Artistique de la Ville de Paris et Société d'Histoire et d'Archéologie du VII Arrondissement, 1981), pp. 64–74.

3. O. Sébastiani, in the exhibition catalogue *Don Quichotte vu par un peintre au XVIII siècle, Natoire* (Compiègne-Aix-en-Provence, 1977), pp. 12–13.

4. Baulez, *La rue de Varenne*, p. 66.

5. Ibid., p. 67.

6. Jean-François Méjanès, in the exhibition catalogue *Les collections du comte d'Orsay: dessins du Musée du Louvre: LXXVIII exposition du Cabinet des dessins* [The Collections of the comte d'Orsay: drawings from the Louvre museum: LXXVIII exhibition of the drawing collection], (Paris: Ministère de la Culture, Éditions de la Réunion des musées nationaux, 1983). The count brought back from Italy some architectural models that are still extant today. See J.-R. Gaborit, "Enquête: les maquettes d'architecture—Répertoire," *Revue de l'art*, no. 58–59 (1983), pp. 123–41.

7. Marquis de Bombelles, *Journal* (edition of Comte Clam Martinic, J. Grassion, and F. Durif), vol. 3 (Geneva, 1993), p. 11.

8. The salon was given this name in a document dated, according to the revolutionary calendar, Germinal 2 year III (2 March 1794) (Archives nationales O^2 436 [87]), *"Quatrième pièce Salon dorré avec pilastres"* (Fourth room Salon doré with pilasters).

9. The dimensions of the mirrors are given in the *inventaire des meubles et effets de la maison d'Orsay*, Germinal 2 year III (2 March 1794) (Archives nationales O^2 436 [87]).

10. The work dates to 1767, but the engraving was announced in the September 1770 issue of *Mercure de France*, p. 176.

11. Christie's, London, 10 December 1992, nos. 402–403, and Sotheby's, New York, 13 October 1983, no. 379 (the four consoles). The table was separated from the rest after having been part of the Béhague collection. It was sold from the collection of Mrs. Anna Thomson Dodge of Rose Terrace, Michigan, by Christie's on 27 September 1971, no. 12.

12. A.-C. Gruber, "Les Vauxhalls parisiens au XVIII siècle," *Bulletin de la Société de l'histoire de l'art français* (1971), pp. 125–34.

13. J. Wilhelm, "La coupole peinte par Antoine Callet pour le salon de compagnie des petits appartements du Palais Bourbon," *Bulletin de la Société de l'histoire de l'art français* (1980), pp. 167–77.

14. Christian Baulez found mention of 5,994 *livres* paid in 1771 to Elie Janel by Chalgrin for work done in the hôtel on the rue de Varenne (Archives nationales, Minutier central LXXXVIII, 730). See Baulez, *La rue de Varenne*, p. 72. The document suggested Chalgrin's involvement in the renovation. The attribution to Chalgrin became certain when it was found that Duret collaborated on the sculptures of the salon. See Bruno Pons, "Un collaborateur de Chalgrin, François-Joseph Duret (1729–1816), Son livre journal de 1767 à 1806," *Bulletin de la Société de l'histoire de l'art français* (1986), p. 138 and cat. no. 35, n. 35.

Elie Janel, a descendant of a Strasbourg coachmaker, seems to have been working as a sculptor while he remained active as a coachmaker. Duret and Janel worked together on the sculptures of the hôtel du Châtelet.

15   They are also fairly similar to those executed for Boullée by Gilles-Paul Cauvet, a sculptor with whom he consistently collaborated.

16   Before the paneling of the Salon Doré was dismantled, a plaster copy was made and installed in its place. It is still in the hôtel de Clermont.

17   The drawings in the Archives nationales have been identified and published by M. Gallet in the *Bulletin du Musée Carnavalet* (1960), and Svend Eriksen, *Early Neo-Classicism in France* (London, 1974), figs. 68, 69.

18   For a drawing in the University Library of Warsaw see Eriksen, *Early Neo-Classicism,* fig. 70. Another drawing is in the collection of James A. de Rothschild at Waddesdon Manor.

19   F. Magny, *Le Palais Bourbon* (Paris, 1987), p. 37.

20   *L'Avant-coureur,* 21 March 1768.

21   The ceiling moved to the hôtel Veil-Picard was completely destroyed in 1970; see Wilhelm, "Deux plafonds peints par Taraval." The date of the Salon exhibition slightly contradicts the dating of the decoration established from the dates the contractors worked at the hôtel d'Orsay. Taraval exhibited the sketch at the Salon of 1773 and, in fact, did not exhibit anything at the Salon of 1771, probably because he was overextended. Thus, the dating of the ceiling to 1770–71 remains highly plausible.

22   This ceiling is described by Hector Chaussier in *Programme des jeux gymniques ouverts à Paris rue de Varenne, numéro 667,* Paris, year VI [1797] (Bibliothèque nationale, printed materials, Vz 1249): "Fourth room. The only thing worthy of any interest in the next room is a ceiling by Taraval, it is without pretension but tasteful, representing a sky and clouds amongst which a few putti are playing."

23   Bombelles, *Journal.*

24   Archives nationales, Minutier central LXXXVIII, 739 bis, 28 February 1774.

25   Now in the Wallace Collection F. 102, no. 204; see Peter Hughes, *Wallace Collection Catalogue: Furniture,* vol. 2 (London, 1996), pp. 1032–43.

26   P. Rémy, *Catalogue des tableaux, groupes et figures de bronze qui composent le cabinet de feu M. Gaignat* (Paris, 1768), no. 62 (auction held in 1769). The copy illustrated by Gabriel de Saint-Aubin is in the Bibliothèque d'art et d'archéologie, Fondation J. Doucet, and is reproduced by E. Dacier in *Catalogues de ventes et livrets de Salon illustrés par Gabriel de Saint-Aubin,* T. XI (Paris, 1921), p. 74. For the sculptures attributed to Desjardins in Hébert's *Dictionnaire pittoresque et historique* (Paris, 1766), p. 115 ("They are thought to be by Desjardins") see F. Souchal, *French Sculptors, The Reign of Louis XIV* (Oxford, England, 1993), T. IV, pp. 16–17, no. 32 bis. They were identified by Christian Baulez and are now at Windsor Castle, Collection of Her Majesty the Queen of England.

27   No mention of the candelabra appears in the 1774 inventory, but they had been placed on the corner consoles by the time of the Revolution. See Archives nationales O^2 436 (87) and F^{17} 1269/10, report of Floréal 27, year II (27 April 1793).

28   Svend Eriksen, *Louis Delanois* (Paris, 1968), p. 52, commission of 28 July 1768. Delanois had just delivered to Warsaw sofas and armchairs commissioned by the king of Poland, the carving of which had been entrusted to Coulonjon. Armchairs designed by Jean-Louis Prieur in 1766 for the Warsaw Palace (see Eriksen, *Louis Delanois,* pls. XXVI, XXVII) included garlands in gilded wood at the seat base that resemble those on the mirrors of the hôtel d'Orsay. They could provide an idea of the design of the Orsay chairs.

29   L.-V. Thiéry, *Guide des amateurs et voyageurs étrangers à Paris* (Paris, 1787), T. II, p. 566.

30   Baulez, *La rue de Varenne,* p. 70.

31   Theodore Sizer, ed., *The Autobiography of John Trumbull, Patriot-Artist 1756–1843* (New Haven, 1953), p. 105.

32   See *Catalogue d'une précieuse et riche collection de tableaux des trois écoles provenant du cabinet du comte d'Orsay* (auction of 14 April 1790); *Catalogue des statues et groupes de marbre antique, figures de bronze, bustes sur leur gaine, vases et colonnes de marbre et autres effets de curiosités appartenant à M. d'Orsay* (auction of 12 September 1791); and

Catalogue d'une riche et précieuse collection de tableaux, qui composait autrefois le cabinet de M. le comte d'Orsay (auction of 20 March 1810).

33   Chaussier, *Programme des jeux gymniques* (1797).

34   Ibid.

35   Because of exceptional circumstances, we do not have a detailed inventory until 1905.

36   Archives nationales I AP 512–515. Emile Peyre, a decorator and antique dealer, bequeathed his collections to the Union centrale des arts décoratifs in 1905. Few details are known of this man, except that he served as a manager at the former hôtel de l'Impératrice, later the hôtel of the baron de Hirsch at 2, rue de l'Elysée. He was also an intermediary in the sale of the dining room groups by Clodion in the hôtel Botterel-Quintin. Peyre's intervention may have been a factor in the decision to make a copy of the salon and to remove its decoration.

37   In 1928, Senator Clark's daughter, Mrs. Marius de Brabent, declared that the salon had been purchased from the duc de La Trémoille We do not know if ancient paneling existed in his hôtel on the avenue Gabriel. By contrast, around 1892 the son of the duc de La Trémoille remounted some ancient paneling in another hôtel (the embassy of the former Yugoslavia). Was a copy of the salon executed during the dismantling of the decor? It is rather surprising to see the painted ceilings removed from the hôtel and replaced by other paintings.

38   *New York Times*, 28 February 1904, sec. 3, p. 1.

39   The table decorated with bronze ornaments by Gouthière was identified by Christian Baulez; see Theodore Dell, *The Frick Collection, vol. 6, Furniture and Gilt Bronzes* (Princeton, 1992), pp. 104–16.

40   M. Sandoz, "Hugues Taraval," *Bulletin de la Société de l'histoire de l'art français* (Paris, 1972), pp. 195–255.

The Salon Doré in America: History and Restoration

DARE MYERS HARTWELL

THE CLARK MANSION

Senator William Andrews Clark (1839–1925) purchased the comtesse d'Orsay's Salon Doré to be the "grand salon" in the house he was building on Fifth Avenue at Seventy-seventh Street in New York City (fig. 19). This was the house that, as it was nearing completion in 1908, the *New York Times* called "New York's Most Expensive Private Mansion."[1] It stood nine stories tall, from the Turkish baths in the sub-basement to the laundry under the eaves, and it contained more than one hundred rooms. The planning and construction took an unprecedented number of years, and it appears to have formed the focal point of Senator Clark's energy and collecting activities.

Clark acquired the property on Fifth Avenue in 1895 and engaged the French architect Henri Deglane (1855–1931), who is best known for the Grand Palais in Paris, to design the house. The New York architectural firm of Lord, Hewlett and Hull carried out the design and adapted the plan for the house to a somewhat enlarged site after Senator Clark decided that there was insufficient

space for his art gallery.[2] Exactly how much of the final appearance of the house was due to Deglane and how much to the American architectural firm is unclear, but it is indisputable that Senator Clark wanted the architecture to be French. An article in the *New York Times* in 1899 states that Clark and Austin W. Lord, a partner in the New York architectural firm, had been in Paris making a study of Parisian architecture and that "Mr. Clark wanted a home after the French style. The house will be of the general Louis XIII style, but so modified as to be little different from modern French."[3]

Although Clark made his fortune in banking, mining, and railroads in Montana and other parts of the American West, from the late 1870s onwards he and his family took many trips to Europe. He was particularly attracted to France, where in later years he spent more and more time. Not surprisingly, this American millionaire wanted to erect a "French palace" on Fifth Avenue.

And a veritable palace it was.[4] The house consisted of two main pavilions united by a domed tower with a cupola. The most important reception rooms were located on the second floor. Here, the tower contained a vaulted rotunda that was thirty-six feet high, with white marble walls and eight Brèche violette marble columns. In the center stood a statue of Venus after the Italian sculptor Antonio Canova (1757–1822; fig. 20). Radiating out from the rotunda were the marble hall, the dining room, the conservatory, and the main picture gallery. This dining room, paneled with English oak carved in the style of Henry IV, was in the southeast corner of the house, and next to it along the Seventy-seventh Street side was the conservatory, visible on the facade as a glass-and-bronze bay above the entrance. The main picture gallery, measuring ninety-five by twenty feet, had skylights and velvet-covered walls. In addition, two other exhibition areas were on this floor, the east gallery and the long gallery, all of which were used to display Senator Clark's collection of Old Master drawings and paintings, eighteenth-century English portraits, and works by nineteenth-century French painters of the Barbizon school, most notably Jean-Baptiste Camille Corot (1796–1875; fig. 21). The exhibition of his vast collection in galleries, rather than in the traditional domestic arrangement, is one of the many unique features of Senator Clark's residence.

In the southwest corner of the house was the "grand salon" into which was placed the paneling from the comtesse d'Orsay's eighteenth-century Salon Doré and the ceiling painting from an adjacent room in the hôtel d'Orsay (figs. 25–27). Although no longer on the ground floor, as it had been in Paris, the wall of French windows on Fifth Avenue continued to look out on a garden setting, in this case, Central Park.

Adjacent to the grand salon was the "petit salon," a gilded room in the style of Louis XV (fig. 22). Its paneling was a pastiche of elements copied from the hôtel de Soubise in Paris.[5] The elliptical shape of the room was reflected in the curve on the west side of the Seventy-seventh Street facade. Beyond the petit salon was the morning room, paneled in dark wood with gold highlights on the carving and inset with four eighteenth-century *portières des dieux* tapestries woven at the Gobelins factory (fig. 23).

Among the rooms on the ground floor were Senator Clark's office suite furnished in the French Empire style, a Gothic-style great hall for smoking and billiards, and the Faience Gallery. The great hall contained a series of six paintings on the life of Joan of Arc commissioned by Senator Clark from the French artist Louis-Maurice Boutet de Monvel (1850–1913), four early sixteenth-century tapestries depicting hunting and pastoral scenes (after designs by Jean Perréal), and a thirteenth-century stained glass window

FIGURE 21

A picture gallery in the Clark residence. The Corcoran Gallery and School of Art Archives.

FIGURE 22

The "petit salon" in the Clark residence. The Corcoran Gallery and School of Art Archives.

from the cathedral at Soissons in France. In the Faience Gallery were exhibited Senator Clark's collections of Greek antiquities, Delft, maiolica, and Palissy ware. Hanging above the exhibition cases were smaller Polonaise and Persian rugs (fig. 24). A separate entrance to the gallery allowed the general public to be admitted to view the collection without walking through the house.

On the third floor was a library with an antique fireplace "taken from an old Normandy castle," a ceiling "transported from an old castle in France," and a stained and enameled glass window by Jean de Caumont depicting scenes from the life of St. Norbert, part of a series commissioned in 1643 for the cloister of the Premonstratensian abbey of Parc in Louvain, Belgium. A breakfast room paneled in English oak carved in the style of Francis I, an "Oriental Room" containing furniture and decorative objects primarily from China and Japan, and a room displaying works by French painter Adolphe Monticelli (1824–1886) completed the third floor.

In addition to these reception rooms, the house contained bedroom suites for Senator and Mrs. Clark and their two daughters, numerous guest rooms (most with private baths), storage rooms for art, accommodations for at least eighteen servants, an elevator large enough for twenty passengers, and on the lower levels, the kitchen and a massive engineering plant.

The exterior of the house was complete by 1907, but the furnishings were still not in place the following year, and the house does not seem to have been occupied until 1912. The cause of this delay is not entirely clear, but apparently the paneling and furnishings

FIGURE 24

The Faience Gallery of the Clark residence. The senator's collection of Greek antiquities, Persian rugs, and maiolica, pictured here, are now in the Corcoran Gallery of Art. The Corcoran Gallery and School of Art Archives.

were being installed between 1907 and 1912. With much of Senator Clark's collection on view at the Corcoran Gallery during the construction of his house, the director's correspondence file provides a few tantalizing glimpses of this process. In January 1910, for example, the Gobelins tapestries were returned to New York for installation in the morning room, but the walls for the paintings had not yet been covered with the sixteenth-century velvet that Clark had purchased for that purpose. Another year passed before the paintings were returned to him, and another sixteen months went by before he wrote to Frederick McGuire on 1 May 1912, "I have everything now fairly well installed both in the way of furnishings and the arrangement of the pictures, tapestries, etc."[6]

It is also apparent from comparing the final inventory with early descriptions of the house that major changes were made in certain areas during this period. In one of the picture galleries, for instance, a stage, fully equipped with dressing rooms and storage area for scenery, could be lowered or raised by hydraulic lift for theatrical performances. It had been installed for Senator Clark's daughter Mary, who enjoyed amateur theatricals, but the stage was removed before the house was occupied. Similarly, Senator Clark initially included two apartments for his married children by his first wife. Both apartments had their own sitting room, dining room, and pantry, and yet both are missing from the final inventory, presumably having been converted to other uses.[7]

Senator Clark died at his home on 2 March 1925 at the age of eighty-six. His will stipulated that his vast collection was to go to the Metropolitan Museum of Art. The bequest, however, carried certain restrictions that board members of the Metropolitan felt they could not meet, and the collection went instead to Senator Clark's alternate choice, the Corcoran Gallery of Art. Clark had enjoyed a long relationship with the Corcoran, beginning in 1901 when he came to Washington as a United States senator. The following year he placed on loan there his enormous painting *The Trial of Queen Katharine* by American artist Edwin Austin Abbey (1852–1911). Eventually, more of his paintings and tapestries were exhibited at the Corcoran while his grand house in New

York was being constructed. Senator Clark was particularly interested in the Corcoran's Biennial Exhibition of Contemporary American Oil Paintings, and he provided money for prizes from its inception in 1907 onwards. He served as a trustee of the Corcoran from 1914 until his death.

In addition to Senator Clark's paintings, sculptures, tapestries, rugs, lace, antiquities, and Delft, maiolica, and Palissy ware, some of the decoration and furnishings from the house also came to the Corcoran. Most notable among these were the Salon Doré and its New York furnishings, but his generosity also included a suite of eight chairs and two sofas designed by English architect Robert Adam (1728–1792) from the "petit salon"; a French Empire suite of three chairs and a sofa from Senator Clark's office area; the mantel and the stained glass window depicting St. Norbert from the library; and the thirteenth-century stained glass window from the cathedral at Soissons in the Gothic billiards room. The latter three elements are now part of the architecture of the Corcoran's galleries in the Clark wing, which was erected by the senator's wife and daughters to house his collection. Even though Clark's New York residence contained many rooms that were created to suggest specific architectural styles, apparently most of the décor was reproduction. The furnishings mentioned above were listed specifically in Senator Clark's will as museum bequests, and therefore they must have been generally recognized as authentic and important pieces. Presumably, all of the rest of the interior decoration, including the Louis XV-style "petit salon," was demolished with the house in 1927.

The Salon Doré in New York

Eighteenth-century French paneling has always been perceived as being movable since the panels were created in workshops and then transported to their intended destination. Obviously, a painting on canvas is even more movable, although a greater difficulty is presented once it is glued to a ceiling. Dismantling interior decoration was therefore not an unusual practice in France, and in fact many of the hôtels in the faubourg Saint-Germain have lost their eighteenth-century décor. In some cases this décor was preserved by moving it to other houses, either in Paris, as occurred with the original Salon Doré ceiling mural, or to another country entirely, as happened with the salon's paneling.

The circumstances surrounding the sale and purchase of the comtesse d'Orsay's Salon Doré are regrettably obscure, but Senator Clark clearly purchased the room before February 1904, when its future installation was described in an article in the *New York Times*.[8] This serves as proof that the room was sold by the Duchâtel family well before the hôtel was purchased in 1905. The fact that the dimensions of the grand salon were determined by the ceiling mural would actually argue for the room's purchase in the early design phase of Clark's house.

It seems unlikely, however, that Senator Clark bought the Salon Doré directly from the Duchâtel family. A note in the Corcoran Gallery's accession file states: "Mrs. Marius de Brabent [Mary Clark], the daughter of Senator Clark stated to the Director of the Gallery on 4 April 1928, that Senator Clark acquired the Louis XVI Salon from le Duc de la Tremoille, either from his Chateau or his Paris Mansion." The duc de La Tremoille was the son-in-law of the comtesse Duchâtel, and he might have represented the family in the sale, but since the Clark family apparently did not know the name or location of the hôtel, it seems likely that Senator Clark actually purchased the room from a dealer. Even more regrettably, it is unlikely that he knew the history of the Salon Doré and the comte and comtesse d'Orsay.

Why Senator Clark purchased the ceiling mural from an adjacent room in the hôtel instead of the Salon Doré ceiling mural is also not known. Both paintings were done by Hugues Taraval at about the same time. The painting originally in the Salon Doré depicted *The Apotheosis of Psyche,* in which Cupid presents Psyche to various gods and goddesses who are arranged on clouds (fig. 15). The adjacent room was larger and more rectangular in shape, and for this ceiling Taraval painted a sky with putti carrying garlands of flowers. At the center of each of the four sides were allegorical figures, representing the Seasons and the Arts, painted to simulate stone sculpture (pl. 22). In Senator Clark's grand salon the mural was oriented so that Autumn and Winter were at the north end of the room above the mantel.

Quite possibly *The Apotheosis of Psyche* had already been sold to Monsieur Veil-Picard for his hôtel in Paris. A more likely explanation, however, for Senator Clark's purchase of the other painting is that he wanted a larger room, and he therefore decided to adapt the gilded paneling to the format of the larger ceiling. (His readiness to do this might argue that the paneling was already dismantled when he first saw it.)

To make the paneling fit the new ceiling, existing elements had to be rearranged and new ones added, including two additional windows, a glass-paned double door, two trophy panels, and four pilasters. A new plaster cornice and plaster capitals for all the pilasters were also made, since the original cornice and capitals in wood had remained in the hôtel d'Orsay.

In its new installation, the room was a long rectangle that ran parallel to Fifth Avenue, and the trophies, mirrors, and doors were not arranged with the same rigorous concern for symmetry as they had been in the hôtel d'Orsay.[9] At the north end of the room stood the fireplace, with a mantel made of marble from Senator Clark's Maryland quarry (fig. 25).[10] This wall followed the format of the hôtel d'Orsay in that one of the mirrors hung over the mantel and on each side of the fireplace was a double door

FIGURE 26

The south (left) and west window walls of the Salon Doré in the Clark residence. The Corcoran Gallery and School of Art Archives.

FIGURE 27

The east wall of the Salon Doré in the Clark residence. The Corcoran Gallery and School of Art Archives.

painted with floral motifs. The two trophies that originally flanked the mantel, however, were moved to the long side walls. The matching doors and mirror were not symmetrically aligned on the opposite wall, but rather a central window overlooking Seventy-seventh Street was inserted there, with a mirror to each side (fig. 26). The west wall contained three windows overlooking Central Park and four trophy panels, with Love in the southwest corner and Victory in the northwest corner. The two trophy panels that had been made for Senator Clark were placed between the windows. Just as the comte d'Orsay's trophy panels reflected his interests in love, victory, music, and the arts and sciences, these new trophies, representing theater and sports, quite likely reflected the interests of Senator Clark and his family (pls. 28, 30–33, cover).

Punctuating the east wall was the second set of painted floral doors (fig. 27). In the southeast corner next to one of these doors was the trophy panel of Arts and Sciences and in the northeast corner next to the other door appeared Music. On the opposite side of each door was a mirror, and between the mirrors was the glass-paned double door that had been made for Senator Clark. At this time the glass in the mirrors, which according to the 1795 inventory was originally in four sections, may have been replaced with single sheets. This was probably considered an advancement when it became possible to obtain single sheets of glass in very large sizes. The green marble baseboard was also probably added in New York. In eighteenth-century France the baseboards were finished in *faux marbre* (wood painted to look like marble) to match the marble of the mantel.

Surprisingly for a house that was extensively covered by the press, no mention is made of the designer who reconfigured the Salon Doré. He was likely someone who functioned as both a dealer and a decorator in France and the United States. With the inclusion of period rooms being a popular affectation for the wealthiest of American residences, this type of business flourished around the turn of the century. The most prominent of the dealer/decorators was Jules Allard (1831–1907), a Parisian who specialized in importing and adapting French interiors as well as making period reproductions. Allard designed all the high style French rooms in the Vanderbilt mansions in New York and Newport, Rhode Island, and along the Hudson River, including a Louis XV-style room for Mrs. William K. Vanderbilt at 660 Fifth Avenue (1883) and a Louis XV-inspired ballroom for Cornelius Vanderbilt II at 1 West Fifty-seventh Street (1892). The John and Mable Ringling Museum of Art in Sarasota, Florida, has two comparable rooms by Allard —one Louis XV and one Regency—from the house of Mrs. William B. Astor located at 840 Fifth Avenue (1895). Likewise, the Museum of Fine Arts in Boston owns a French salon he made for the home of William Salomon at 1020 Fifth Avenue (1904). At The Breakers in Newport, the summer "cottage" of Cornelius Vanderbilt II, Allard reused some period items in the interior decorations, among them the paneling from a circa 1778 salon attributed to Gilles-Paul Cauvet from the hôtel Mégret Sérilly, Paris. Installed in the ladies drawing room in 1895, Allard reworked and "improved upon" the paneling to suit American aesthetic ideas.[11]

While no documentary evidence links Senator Clark and Allard, the quality of the workmanship of the elements that were added to the Salon Doré paneling, particularly the two new trophy panels, does suggest that Allard and his workshop might have been responsible for the room's adaptation. The adjacent Louis XV "petit salon," a complete reproduction, also points to the involvement of a person such as Allard.

When finally installed, Senator Clark's grand salon was opulently furnished. Arranged around the room were a set of two sofas, two love seats, and eight chairs upholstered with eighteenth-century Beauvais tapestries mounted on modern gilded wood frames. Two inlaid wood commodes (or chest of drawers) with Brèche violette marble tops, one by Pierre-Antoine Foullet (ca. 1732–ca. 1780) dating circa 1770 and the other a late nineteenth-century copy of a piece by Jean-Henri Riesener, were placed under the mirrors on the east wall. Also in the room were a cabinet with glass doors bordered by a painted paper frieze with Pompeiian designs, and a harpsichord decorated with painted roses and putti, made in 1770 by Jean-Mari Dedeban in Paris. The room was lit by sixteen electrified sconces with silk shades mounted on the pilasters and by two electrified candelabra on top of gilded wood *torchères*.

On the mantel stood gilded bronze candelabra and a clock, carried by two Roman vestals, made for the boudoir (private sitting room) of Marie-Antoinette in the Tuileries Palace (pl. 39). Gilded bronze andirons, dated circa 1770–75, with a classical altar at the top and the head of Medusa on the base, enlivened the fireplace. Several marble and gilded bronze figurines were scattered about the room.

Above the windows were curtain rods festooned with gilded garlands that roughly continued the garland motif from the top of the mirrors around the room. Beneath them hung tapestry *cantonnières,* a kind of valance with sides hanging down the wall. The design on the *cantonnières* appears to have been a trompe l'oeil blue drapery swag with flowers and simulated tassels and fringe. The top layer of curtains were a cut-velvet design of garlands, plants in urns (remarkably similar to the lower door panels), and

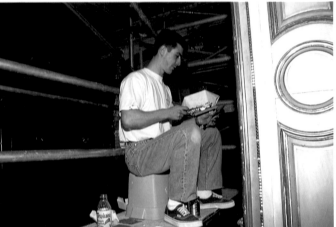

PLATE 8 (LEFT)

Philippe Equy recutting the gesso on Sports, *one of two trophy panels made for Senator Clark.*

PLATE 9 (RIGHT)

Hervé Gehler applying gold leaf.

small-scale garden tools on an ivory background (pl. 7). Underneath were several layers of lace and batiste curtains as well as linen window shades. Lace panels covered the glass panes in the double door. Several Persian rugs were on the floor.[12]

Senator Clark purchased all these furnishings from varying sources, and with the exception of the *torchères*, which are said to have belonged to the Duchâtel family, there is no reason to connect any of them with the hôtel d'Orsay.

Technique and Technical Analysis

The Clark additions to the paneling tend to be more robust and broadly carved than the original eighteenth-century elements. It is also possible to distinguish these two periods through a microscopic examination of cross sections of the gilding, which clearly show each layer in a given area. Eighteenth-century French gilding techniques, many of which are still practiced today, had been refined since the early seventeenth century and involved very specific materials, techniques, and skills that were acquired only over a long apprenticeship. Briefly, the steps involved in this process are as follows: Numerous layers of liquid gesso (a mixture of glue size and chalk) were applied to panels carved in the workshop of the *menuisier* (carpenter) and the *sculpteur* (carver). After the gesso was smoothed and polished, the most highly skilled craftsmen recut in the gesso details that were outlined in the carving (pl. 8). This was done with recutting irons, hook-shaped tools that cut on the pull stroke. As artistic styles changed in France, so did the characteristic strokes and patterns of recutting. This recutting (*reparure*) in the gesso is responsible for the fineness of the detail in the original Salon Doré paneling. Look, for example, at the hat in Love (pl. 4) and the plumed helmet and shield (pl. 1) and the fish-shaped bugle and quiver in Victory (pl. 44).

After the recutting was completed, yellow ochre pigment mixed with glue size was brushed into the interstices to cover the white gesso in case breaks occurred in the gold leaf in these hard-to-gild areas. A layer of bole, a very fine clay mixed with glue size, was then applied to the areas to be gilded. Together the bole and the gesso formed a smooth, pliant bed for the gold leaf, which was applied after the substrate was moistened with water (hence the term "water gilding"[pl. 9]). More than one color of gold leaf was some-times used. Two colors—yellow gold and, for the highlights, a "green gold" that derives its color from its silver content—were utilized in the Salon Doré. In the final step of the process, details were highlighted by burnishing the gold with an agate stone. Other areas

PLATE 10

1.
2.

3.

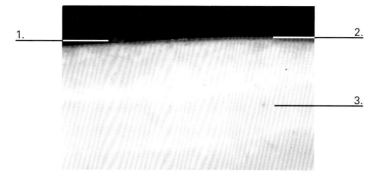

A. Magnification 400x.

1.
2.

3.

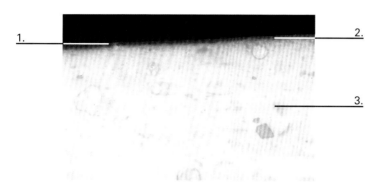

B. Magnification 400x.

1.
2.

3.

4.

5.

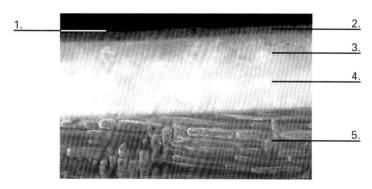

C. Magnification 400x.

1.
3.
5.
7.
9.
11.
13.
14.

2.
4.
6.
8.
10.
12.

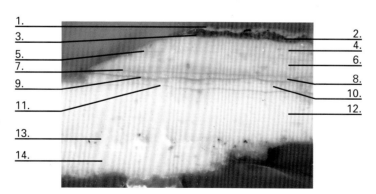

D. Magnification 200x.

A. OLD GILDING I.

Sample taken from tassel of Arts and Sciences trophy.

1. Gilding (1 micron).

2. Bole (8 microns).

3. Gesso (greater than 1 mm). Fossils are not visible in this section of the sample.

B. OLD GILDING II.

Sample taken from tassel of Arts and Sciences trophy.

1. Gilding (too abraded to be visible here).

2. Bole (8 microns).

3. Gesso (greater than 1 mm). The spherical shapes in the gesso ground are fossils.

C. CLARK GILDING.

Sample taken from a pilaster.

1. Gilding (1–2 microns).

2. Bole (16 microns).

3. Upper gesso layer (72 microns).

4. Lower gesso layer (64 microns).

5. Wood substrate.

D. WALL PAINT.

Sample taken from the background of Music trophy.

1. Yellowish gray paint, probably synthetic (24 microns).

2. Resinous pigmented layer (2–24 microns).

3. Dirt.

4. Grayish white oil paint (52 microns).

5. Dirt.

6. Yellowish white oil paint (52 microns).

7. Dirt or an air gap.

8. White paint: chalk in a glue binder (12–20 microns).

9. Shellac?

10. White paint or gesso: chalk in a glue binder (24–36 microns).

11. Shellac.

12. Thick white paint or ground layer: fossiliferous chalk and lead white in a glue binder (ca. 120 microns).

13. Bluish white paint consisting of lead white, chalk, an organic blue colorant, and charcoal black, the pigments for *blanc de roi* (ca. 40 microns).

14. Gesso: fossiliferous chalk in a glue binder (ca. 84 microns).

PLATE 10

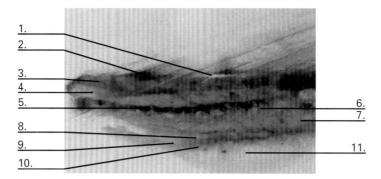

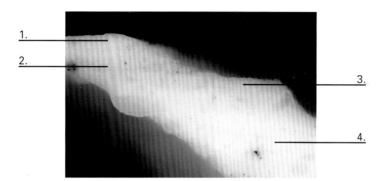

E. Magnification 250x.

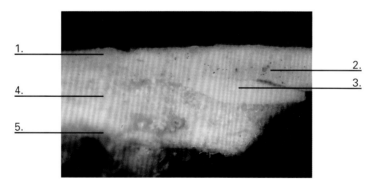

F. Magnification 100x.

G. Magnification 100x.

E. GREEN STEM

From top right panel of door on the north side of mantel.

1. Varnish (ca. 9 microns).

2. Blue-green paint (ca. 24 microns).

3. Blue-green paint (ca. 24 microns).

4. Pale blue-green paint (ca. 40 microns).

5. Dark blue-green paint (ca. 18 microns).

6. Yellow paint (ca. 18 microns).

7. Pale blue-green paint (ca. 24 microns).

8. Pale blue-green paint (ca. 24 microns).

9. Natural resin coating (ca. 15 microns).

10. Pale blue-green paint (ca. 24 microns).

11. White ground (ca. 75 microns). The binder for the paint and ground layers is oil except for layer 3, which is shellac. Layer 10 is probably the original paint surface.

F. CEILING MURAL

Original paint taken from proper right arm of putto with wreaths.

1. Pale flesh-toned highlight (ca. 15 microns).

2. Pink flesh (ca. 15 microns).

3. Blue sky composed of lead white with a small amount of Prussian blue (ca. 20 microns).

4. White ground layer (>250 microns). (SEM-EDS actually distinguishes three layers of ground: 1. Lead white [100 microns]; 2. Chalk/lead white [55 microns]; 3. Chalk with a small amount of lead white [>100 microns]. A little charcoal is also present.) The binder for the paint and ground layers is oil. A thin layer of glue over the canvas, which appears in other cross sections of the original paint, may have been missed in the sampling.

G. CEILING MURAL

Paint from sky, north side of fireplace.

1. Blue-gray layer containing ultramarine, chromium oxide green, and yellow iron oxides (22–38 microns).

2. Pinkish brown layer (30–45 microns).

3. Fragment of lead white in oil (0–45 microns).

4. 100% chalk and oil ground (100 microns).

5. Glue layer (20 microns).

received a matte finish created with a light coating of glue size. These refinements in the use of gold leaf made French artisans the preeminent gilders in eighteenth-century Europe (pl. 11).

Analysis of samples taken from both the original salon elements and the Clark additions reveals the composition of the gold leaf and the bole to be remarkably similar. Pure gold with a trace of iron was used for most of the gilding; gold leaf containing a small amount of silver and sometimes traces of iron or copper was used for the green gold highlights. The bole is a fine-grained orange clay matrix with particles of hematite and charcoal, which give it a dark red color. Despite these similarities, significant differences are found when cross sections of the surface coatings are examined under the microscope (pls. 10A, B, C). On the original elements the bole is extremely thin, varying from 3 to 16 microns and averaging 6.4 microns, whereas on the Clark additions it is relatively thick, ranging from 14 to 55 microns and averaging 27.6 microns. Furthermore, although the whiting in both gessoes is calcite, on the original elements it is fossiliferous and was applied in multiple layers with indistinct boundaries. With a few exceptions, on the Clark additions it was applied in two distinct layers and contains no fossils. The exceptions are samples taken from a plaster capital and the Clark trophies, which have a fossiliferous gesso ground.[13]

It is evident that high-quality materials were used for the Clark additions to emulate the original elements as closely as possible. The plaster cornice and capitals were probably cast in Paris from the originals in the hôtel d'Orsay, and the new elements could also have been carved there. Quite likely, however, the additions were actually gilded in New York, probably after the room was installed. This would have been the most sensible approach, since surface damage was likely to occur in shipment, and areas of the original paneling would also have required restoration after the trauma of dismantling and reinstallation. What is surprising is that the two Clark trophies did not have recutting in the gesso, and green gold was applied in a manner inconsistent with French conventions. Intended for use only for highlights or secondary motifs, the green gold was applied correctly on the ribbons of the stop fluting and the leaves of the trophy panels. In New York, however, more primary motifs, such as some of the flowers on the trophy of Love, were incorrectly restored using green, not yellow, gold leaf (pl. 13), and some of the accoutrements of the Theater panel, one of the trophies made for Senator Clark, were gilded in green gold.

A surfeit of gold leaf also made its way onto the sculpture panels above the doors. Whereas in the hôtel d'Orsay only the ribbons and garlands were gilded, in New York the hair and wings of the putti and the figures in the medallions also were decorated with gold leaf (pl. 17). These anomalies could be attributed to artisans who were not trained in French gilding techniques and conventions, or it could have been a matter of economy and taste. Recutting is an expensive, time-consuming process, and perhaps the designer thought no one in America would notice if it were missing. The application of the gold leaf may have reflected Senator Clark's personal preference, or the designer's perception of the artistic taste of a wealthy American.

The fossiliferous grounds on the plaster capitals and the Clark trophies are somewhat surprising. If they were indeed made in Paris, they could also have received their gesso ground before they were shipped to New York, where they would have been completed. (Although it was possible to purchase fossiliferous gesso in New York, it does not seem likely that a workshop with such consistent habits would change the type of gesso for certain pieces.) Certainly the cross sections indicate that the bole and the gilding on all the Clark additions were applied by the same workshop. The converse of this—that all architectural elements with ground and/or bole from this workshop are Clark additions—does not hold true, as these artisans also carried out a good deal of restoration on the original elements, particularly the pilasters.

More than a hundred samples were taken in 1988 from areas that appeared to contain old or traditional gilding, and the majority of the cross sections follow one of the two types illustrated here. A few isolated examples with unusual layer structures, however, suggest that numerous other, minor treatments also must have occurred over the years.

The ceiling mural is painted in oil on three widths of canvas that run the length of the room (pl. 22). The canvas is glued directly to the plaster, thus making removal extremely difficult. In fact, the canvas suffered significant damage when it was taken off the ceiling of the hôtel d'Orsay. Tears occurred along the edges of all three pieces of canvas, and a large loss in the paint layer in the center of the sky extended from below the central group of putti across the legs of the putto nearest the allegorical figures of Spring and Summer. In New York this loss was filled with a putty and, along with the tears and canvas seams, broadly repainted in an oil-based paint that extended beyond the area of damage. Additionally, the figures of Autumn and Winter may have been completely repainted in a slightly higher position to compensate for the projection of the chimney and cornice in Senator Clark's house. (The chimney and cornice now in the room from which the painting came in the hôtel d'Orsay do not project onto the ceiling.) The parapet is certainly much higher in this area, and the paint layer is dissimilar in color and texture to the other three groups of figures. Cross sections taken from this area did not reveal a lower layer of paint, but this may reflect the difficulty in obtaining a good sample.

The Salon Doré at the Corcoran

T. D. Wadelton of New York City served as the contractor for the removal of the Salon Doré from Senator Clark's house and its reinstallation at the Corcoran. In 1928 he received more than $11,000 for his work. Apparently the removal of the paneling ensued without serious incident, but the difficulties encountered in removing the painting from the ceiling are well documented in a series of telegrams and other forms of correspondence exchanged between C. Powell Minnigerode, Director of the Corcoran, the architect Charles A. Platt, and John H. Hall, Jr., who was married to Senator Clark's granddaughter.[14] On 10 February 1926, Minnigerode wrote to Platt:

> *I have just received the following telegram...*
> *Wadeltons man started removing fragonard ceiling this morning has removed only small section about two feet long by six inches wide and torn it in two places therefore I have stopped work temporarily in order to inform you.[15]*

Following this exchange, a Mr. Humerich, who had originally installed the painting in Senator Clark's house, was brought in to take it down, but he met with no more success. On 13 March 1926, Minnigerode wired Platt:

> *Mr. John H. Hall, Jr., the representative of the Clark Executors at the house, wires me that they are having great difficulty removing Fragonard ceiling, that chips are flaking off with every blow of chisel, that Wadelton and Humerich desire conference with me on Monday, and that work has stopped in the meantime.*

And, even worse, Platt informed Minnigerode on 18 March:

> *Previous to the receipt of your telegram and letter of the 13th Mr. Wadelton reported to me the difficulty they were encountering. Accordingly I arranged to meet Mr. Wadelton at the mansion to reconsider one of the methods we originally advanced; that is, to remove the ceiling in its entirety. We had our meeting Tuesday and decided that this appears to be a practical solution. The idea is to cut the ceiling into sections, painting lath and plaster in a complete slab about one inch thick, pad and box each section and ship the whole thing direct from mansion to the Corcoran Gallery by motor truck, and then re-erect it in place the same way. After it is re-erected touch it up and make good whatever damage has been done to it.*
>
> *Yesterday I got on the track of another combination of men who have taken down and put up a similar ceiling in the gallery in this city. Before trying the method above mentioned, we will confer with this new combination tomorrow or next day.*

Better news finally arrived on 22 March, when Platt wrote to Minnigerode:

> *I had an interview Saturday with Mr. Wadelton and the new man I referred to in my recent letter about taking down the ceiling by the first method that was discussed.*
>
> *They report to me that by inserting a putty knife under the skim coat of plaster they found that the canvas was readily separated from the base plastering and that, apparently, it is still possible to take down the canvas that way. I therefore ordered them to proceed at once with the idea of taking down the canvas and lay it on the floor, at which time we will consult the people who would do the restoring and see what arrangements we can make with them.*

On 2 April, T. D. Wadelton, the contractor, wrote to Platt:

Dear Sir:

The painting has been removed from the ceiling of the Drawing Room in the Clark House at #1 East 77th Street, and is at present laid out on the floor of the picture gallery.

It was found, on taking the picture down, that there were two seams in the width, which came apart, making three widths approximately 7'—9" wide. The removal from the ceiling was accomplished with very little damage to the painting except at the northerly end, where it held particularly fast to the plaster. The damage consists of the scaling off of some of the paint on the large figure and shield at center of north end, and at either side of same, tears and scaling of the paint in the field and border.

It is my opinion. . .that the best procedure was to put the painting on the 12" diameter drums we have made, in its present condition and ship it to Washington by motor truck. On its arrival there it should be laid flat until such time as the new room is ready for it. It would then be put up with white lead and the torn portions be patched and replaced with new canvas where necessary on the ceiling. The cracks would then be filled in with gilders size and then touched up.

The damaged area, now at the west end of the painting above the mantelpiece, includes the figures of Autumn and Winter. After the painting was installed at the Corcoran, these figures were completely overpainted with an oil-based paint to cover the damage (fig. 34). Close examination of a photograph of the room in Senator Clark's house reveals that the repainting did not necessarily follow the earlier design. Drapery was painted over the raised bare leg of Autumn, and what appears to be a brazier beside Winter was overpainted with a bundle of yarn or twigs, and a flint or spindle was placed in her hand. In the medallion between the two figures, a satyr on the left was replaced by a tree. It is not clear why the restorer did not simply follow the original composition, but it may have been easier to hide the damage on the figures with more complicated design elements. Besides, a tree is certainly easier to paint than a satyr.

The canvas seams and both new and old tears were also overpainted at the time of the Corcoran installation, again using a broad manner that extended onto undamaged areas. The colors of the painting had grayed somewhat due to the layers of grime and the oil overpaint, applied in New York, that had darkened in the approximately twenty years since its application. Therefore, the overpainting done in Washington was carried out in colors that matched an altered tonality. An unpigmented oil coating, which at the time of the 1990 restoration covered most of the mural, including the overpainting on the damaged figures of Autumn and Winter, was also almost certainly applied at that time.

The Clark wing of the Corcoran was designed to house the Salon Doré, and no changes were made in the configuration of the paneling when it was moved to Washington. A certain amount of regilding was required in areas where gold leaf and gesso had flaked off. The regilding apparently was done by F. Sampietro of New York City, who also seems to have carried out the restoration of the ceiling mural.[16] Quite likely Sampietro used bronze powder paint instead of gold leaf, a technique that moved him even farther from the original French gilding process than the artisans who carried out the gilding in New York.[17]

PLATE 12

The Salon Doré as it appeared in the 1980s.

At the Corcoran the former south window became the main entryway between the Salon Doré and the adjacent gallery, and the glass doors were mirrored to hide the brick wall behind them. Otherwise the appearance of the room, including the placement of the furniture and decorative objects, remained essentially the same. The Clark wing, including the Salon Doré, opened to the public in 1928.

Restoration

Between 1928 and the 1980s furnishings in the Salon Doré changed very little. At some point the curtains were taken down, probably because the fabric had deteriorated. Lampshades were removed from the electric candlelights on the sconces, and the clock was damaged and replaced by another depicting the Chariot of the Harvest drawn by two panthers.

As time passed, however, the condition of the room deteriorated, primarily due to an early lack of climate control and misguided attempts at conservation and restoration. Few museums had climate control until the second half of this century. Before the museums's installation of air conditioning and humidity controls, Washington's summertime heat and high humidity caused hygroscopic materials such as the wood paneling and the glue in the gesso to expand, while the low humidity inside the building during the wintertime made them contract. Disturbing losses in the gold leaf appeared when areas of

gesso lost their adhesion and eventually began to flake off as the result of this cycle of expansion and contraction (pl. 13). The paint and ground layers on the ceiling mural and the floral door panels were subject to the same problem (fig. 29).

Additionally, the large French windows were often previously left open for ventilation, allowing in dirt and air pollutants from the street, which were then deposited on the walls and ceiling. In eighteenth-century Paris, the flat wall surfaces of the Salon Doré were *blanc de roi*, or "king's white," so called because the color was often used in the king's apartments. A very white, glue-based paint, *blanc de roi* was used primarily in combination with gilding, where its color and matte surface appearance enhanced the sheen of the gold.[18] The cross section of a sample taken from the wall of the Salon Doré in 1988 confirms that the paint layers became progressively darker over the years, the result of painting to match dirty colors (pl. 10D). The exact color of the walls of the Salon Doré in Senator Clark's house and in the early years at the Corcoran is not entirely clear. A 1905 newspaper account describes the walls in both the grand and petit salons as gray, but examination of photographs from the period suggest they were closer to white (pl. 7).[19] By the 1980s, however, the flat wall surfaces in the Salon Doré ranged in tone from gray to ochre, the victim of layers of dirt and numerous retouching efforts (pl. 12). Areas above the dado rail seem to have received the most work: they were considerably darker than the lower section and were particularly marred by localized retouching in oil paint, which darkened in time to become unsightly splotches (pl. 13). The doors remained a cream color, which perhaps was an aged version of the wall color in Senator Clark's house (pl. 17).

Only one major restoration of the gilding is documented. The back of the west side of the mirror-paned double doors bears an inscription in Hungarian: "This hall was restored (that is, only the gilding and the doors have been repaired) twice (during the second half of years 1954 and 1955) by István Pálvölgyi-Pfeiffer/certified artist crafts-

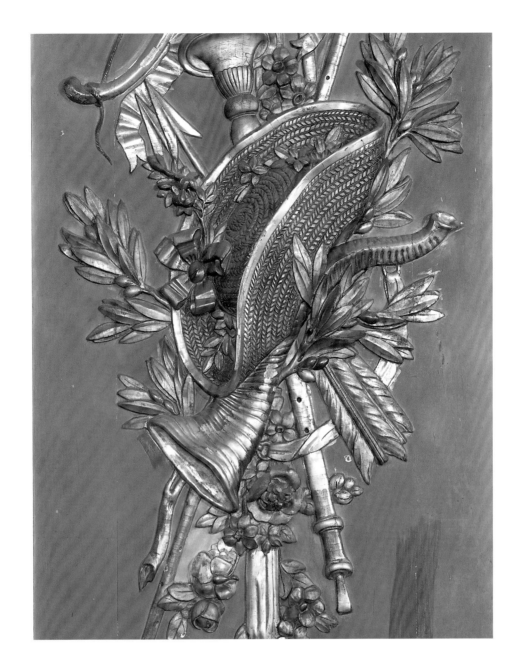

PLATE 13

Detail of trophy panel depicting Love, before treatment. On the gilding, the darker areas are the old gold and the bright areas are restoration. Gold leaf has flaked off in the white areas, leaving the gesso visible. The dark splotches in the painted background are discolored retouching. A small cleaning test can be seen below the horn in the background and on the flower. The leaves are green gold; in addition, some of the flowers have been incorrectly regilded with green gold leaf.

PLATE 14

Detail of trophy panel depicting Love after treatment.

PLATE 15

Detail of central section of Taraval's ceiling mural before treatment.

man."[20] A photograph from the Corcoran registrar's files documents this restoration (fig. 28). On the left is Hermann Warner Williams, Director of the Corcoran (1947–68); in the center, pointing to the flowers on the doors, is presumably Mr. Pálvölgyi-Pfeiffer; and the man at the far right may be James Breckenridge, Keeper of the Clark Collection (1952–55).

It is unclear exactly what is meant by the phrase "restored twice," especially with a period of six months or so indicated in between. Was the work carried out at two separate times for financial or scheduling reasons, or did some problem arise after the first campaign that had to be corrected by a second effort? Whatever the case, this can be considered one major restoration because the same restorer worked over a relatively brief period of time.

By comparing the areas shown undergoing treatment in the photograph with the same areas in the 1980s, it becomes clear that this restoration did not utilize orthodox French materials and methods. Areas in which the gesso had deteriorated and flaked off were generally regessoed with an overly hard material that did not allow the gold leaf to be burnished. In addition, new gesso was not recut, resulting in a loss of detail and definition. Bronze powder paint was used for regilding instead of gold leaf. Perhaps the bronze color matched at the time of its application, but by the 1980s the extensive repairs appeared much brighter than the old gold surrounding them (pl. 13). Varnish had been applied to areas of gilding (perhaps on more than one occasion), probably in an attempt to consolidate the deteriorated gesso. It may have exacerbated the problem, and it certainly sealed in the dirt and dulled all the burnished areas. Gesso and gold leaf continued to flake off, leaving lower layers of white gesso exposed.

Detaching paint posed an ongoing problem for several of the painted floral doors, and judging from this apparently staged photograph, losses in the paint and ground layers were filled and inpainted during this restoration, and perhaps at other times as well. A layer of varnish was found on the doors at the time of the 1989 restoration, and this varnish may also have been applied by Mr. Pálvölgyi-Pfeiffer to consolidate the paint. (Painted door panels in France have a matte appearance and were never varnished, being considered part of the architecture and not easel paintings.) By the 1980s numerous losses marred the paint layer—some exposed the bare wood substrate—and the varnish on the doors had become yellow and grimy (fig. 29; pl. 19).

The ceiling mural had also received intermittent repairs. A synthetic resin varnish found on the surface in localized areas may have been applied as a consolidant for detaching paint, but insecurities in the paint layer continued. Furthermore, the aesthetic appearance of the ceiling had deteriorated as radically as that of the walls. Over the years the painting had acquired a thick layer of grime, the unpigmented oil coating had turned brown, and the overpaint on the seams, tears, and losses had darkened to gray so that storm clouds appeared to hover in the sky (pl. 15).

In 1987, aided by the financial support of the Women's Committee of the Corcoran Gallery of Art, the decision was made to begin researching the history and original appearance of the Salon Doré in the hope that it might be possible to restore it to its early glory. At that time very little was known about either of these areas, and limited information or expertise were available in the United States. Over the next several years the curator of collections and the conservator consulted French, and other, experts, studied eighteenth-century French gilding in and around Paris, visited the hôtel d'Orsay (now called the hôtel

PLATE 16

Detail of the ceiling mural showing the damaged end of the garland, after the removal of grime and the darkened oil coating. The putto's head and torso have been repainted, while the lower part of his body and the garland have been replaced with a gray cloud.

PLATE 17

One of four sets of floral painted doors in the Salon Doré, before treatment.

de Clermont), examined the work of restorers in both the United States and France, and solicited proposals for treatment.[21] Fundraising for the project began during this period, partly in connection with the bicentennial of the French Revolution in 1989.

During this extensive research, the discrepancy between the appearance of the Salon Doré when it was part of a small room in the hôtel d'Orsay and its present incarnation became abundantly clear. Returning the paneling to its original configuration was not a reasonable, or even a desirable, option for the Corcoran, since the space in the Clark wing was built to hold the room as it now appears. Separating the paneling from the ceiling mural would be equally compromising. The present ceiling by Taraval, while not original to the salon, is at least close in style and spirit, if not in size, to the now-destroyed painting. Equally important, Senator Clark is critical to the history of the Corcoran, and his purchase and adaptation of the Salon Doré exemplifies the type of collecting exercised by wealthy Americans at the turn of the century. Indeed, Senator Clark's additions have become an integral part of the salon's history.

Even so, the surface appearance of the paneling and ceiling mural was no longer acceptable, either aesthetically or historically. Restoring the Salon Doré began in earnest in 1989 with the treatment of the painted floral panels on the doors. The restoration of the ceiling mural began soon afterward in 1990, and the treatment of the gilded paneling took place in 1993. Both the painted panels and the ceiling mural were treated by American painting conservators under the direction of the Corcoran's conservator. The restoration of the gilding was carried out by a Parisian firm specializing in eighteenth-century French gilding.

Doors

On the doors the lifting paint of the flowers was reattached by introducing an adhesive under the paint flakes and then pressing them back into place. Solvents were used to remove the yellowed varnish (pl. 19). Losses in the paint layer were filled to surface level and inpainted to match the surrounding area. The retouching paint, prepared by the conservators by grinding dry pigment in a synthetic medium, is easily distinguished chemically from the original and will remain readily soluble should it need to be removed in the future.[22]

The background of the flowers had not discolored to the same extent as the walls, but because it had yellowed with age and was disfigured with dirt, it was repainted along with the surrounding flat paneling. Tiny brushes were used to paint around the flowers, leaves, ribbons, and trailing tendrils. Evidence suggests that past restorers were less scrupulous in their methods. In the flowers a lower layer of paint was sometimes visible under lifting paint flakes, and cross sections made from microscopic samples show multiple paint layers in some areas, an indication that the flowers have been at least partially repainted (pl. 10E). Furthermore, the presence of chrome yellow and chrome green pigments in the upper layers date this repainting to no earlier than 1818, when chrome yellow came into commercial production.[23] Perhaps the doors were repainted during the restoration commissioned by the Duchâtel family after they purchased the house in 1838. Why the doors were repainted is unclear, but the repainting might reflect a desire to give the flowers a more contemporary look.

Ceiling Mural

The first step in restoring the ceiling mural was to reattach loose paint by injecting an adhesive into the affected areas and gently working the paint back into place with a warm tacking iron.[24] Only after this was finished could the difficult task of removing the layers of dirt, varnish, oil, and overpaint begin. Different combinations of solvents were used depending on the nature and age of the layer: the older overpaint applied in New York required stronger solvents than did the overpaint that had been applied at the Corcoran in 1928.

After most of the overpaint was removed, it became possible to assess the true condition of the ceiling painting. In particular, the west end of the painting with the figures of Autumn and Winter was badly damaged in the move to Washington, and the area from below the central putti to the east end of the garland had presumably been damaged when the painting was removed from the hôtel in Paris. Other figures were generally in good condition, although tears and sometimes a slight misalignment in the canvases occurred in those areas where figures run across seams. (Perfect realignment on the ceiling would have been virtually impossible with such large canvases.)

PLATE 22

Composite of the ceiling mural of the Salon Doré after restoration.

Allegorical figures represent the Arts and the Seasons

(clockwise from top): Poetry and Music (north wall); Winter and Autumn (west wall); Painting and Sculpture (south wall); and

Summer and Spring (east wall).

FIGURE 30

Detail of Taraval's ceiling mural showing the allegorical figures of Music (left) and Poetry
after the oil coating and overpaint were removed.

FIGURE 31

Detail of ceiling mural showing Poetry and Music after retouching.

FIGURE 32

Detail of Taraval's ceiling mural showing the allegorical figures of Spring (left) and Summer after the oil coating and overpaint were removed. The two seams in the canvas run vertically through the extremities of the figures; tears in the canvas run perpendicular to the seams.

FIGURE 33

Detail of ceiling mural showing Spring and Summer after retouching.

FIGURE 34

Detail of Taraval's ceiling mural showing the allegorical figures of Autumn (left) and Winter before treatment.

FIGURE 35

Detail of ceiling mural showing Autumn and Winter after restoration.

The paint in the broad expanse of sky differs in color and structure from that immediately surrounding and running under the figures, suggesting that much of the sky has been repainted.[25] A cross section of original paint taken from the arm of the putto with wreaths reveals a thick ground layer of chalk and lead white in oil. Above the ground, the pale blue paint of the sky is composed of lead white with a small amount of Prussian blue. The flesh tones of the putto are painted over the sky, and all the layers are closely bound together, indicating that very little time elapsed between the application of each layer. By contrast, a cross section of repaint from the sky on the north side of the fireplace confirms a completely different structure. Here, the ground is chalk and oil with no lead white; above the ground is a fragment of lead white followed by two layers of paint, the lower being a pinkish brown and the uppermost one a blue gray. This paint, unlike that used for the sky under and around the putti, contains a variety of pigments, including ultramarine, chromium oxide green, and yellow iron oxides. Since hydrated chromium oxide was not available until around 1838, this paint could not be original to the ceiling (pl. 10f, G).[26]

The repainting of certain areas of the sky dates back to the ceiling's installation in the hôtel in Paris. Unlike the repainting undertaken after the two moves, it was not sensitive to solvents, and it was in place when the tears from the first removal occurred. Most likely this repainting took place during the restoration of the hôtel that was undertaken after the Duchâtel family purchased it in 1838. The painting probably sustained significant damage during the hôtel's years of misuse and neglect following the French Revolution. Instead of consolidating and saving flaking paint in the sky, the less time-consuming method of scraping and repainting the area may have been chosen. Fortunately, the restorers seem to have treated the figures with greater respect and care.

The next stage in the restoration was applying a synthetic resin varnish by rubbing it onto the ceiling to bring out the colors of the painting and to isolate the original paint from the retouching. As with the flowers on the doors, the retouching paint was prepared by the conservators by grinding dry pigment in a synthetic medium that will remain readily soluble and will not discolor. In addition to inpainting the tears and losses, old repainted areas and discolorations in the sky were glazed to approximate the original paint color and to smoothe transitions from one area to another. These glazes were made transparent by adding large amounts of retouching medium to the colors which were mixed in a jar. Pads made of cheesecloth-covered cotton balls were used to apply the glaze. For the design elements, inpainting colors were mixed together on the palette and applied with a small brush in the normal retouching manner.[27]

Removal of the overpainted drapery below the proper right hand of Autumn revealed that her right leg was substantially intact, although it was damaged by tears. Unfortunately, the original paint beneath Winter's overpainted bundle of wool or faggots was so badly damaged that it was impossible to determine the original intention. A warming pot of coals appears to be in the photograph of the room installed in New York, but only smokelike vestiges of this paint remain. With so little on which to base a recreation, tears were simply painted over, with the hope that a prototype for Winter's accouterment eventually might be found and the area redone at a later date. The same problem also existed in the medallion, where a satyr on the left had been repainted as a tree at the time of the Corcoran installation. With only traces of original paint remaining, the most recent restoration did not attempt to recreate the satyr (figs. 34, 35).

PLATE 23

Detail of Taraval's ceiling mural during cleaning, showing the putto whose face was disfigured by the torn and misaligned

canvas on the seam.

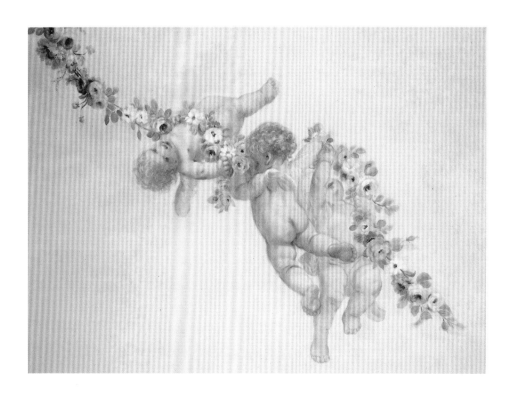

PLATE 24

Detail of Taraval's ceiling mural showing the putto after treatment.

The restoration of the east end of the garland presented the greatest challenge because of the large loss that runs from below the central group of putti across the legs of the putto nearest Spring and Summer. Previous restorers did not recreate this putto's missing legs but rather covered the area with a cloud. The figure's head and torso, however, were heavily repainted using brownish tones in a style that differed markedly from that of the other putti (pls. 15, 16). After this overpaint was removed, the putto's head and torso, though abraded, were found to be intact. As his pose duplicates that of one of the putto at the left end of the central group, it was possible to use this putto for the restoration (pl. 34). A tracing was made of his legs and then transferred to the area of loss by applying paint over holes punched in the tracing paper following the design. His highlighting and shading were then followed in recreating the legs and retouching the upper body.

The east end of the garland also had to be recreated. Tracings made of flowers in the garland to the west of the central putti were assembled into a drawing of a garland that connects the putto in profile to the end putto, where the remains of the tail of the original garland are visible in his proper right hand. The drawing was then transferred to the ceiling in the manner described above, and the flowers were repainted, following the originals as closely as possible. Again, a synthetic retouching medium was used to ensure easy identification and reversibility of the new paint layer.

A putto from the group at the west end of the garland presented another interesting restoration problem. His face runs across the seam and, because of the slight misalignment of the canvases, his eyes were askew. In addition, a section of canvas along the seam that included his nose and mouth had been completely torn away during the removal of the ceiling. After the ceiling was remounted, the detached piece was somewhat larger than the hole it had left. Once it was reset on top of the surrounding canvas, the putto's face was distinctly distorted. To offset these problems, the area had been heavily overpainted—but with no visible improvement (pl. 23). After the overpaint was cleaned away, the torn piece of canvas was removed and adjusted slightly so it fit into the aperture. Losses and seams were then filled and minimally retouched. Although the putto is still somewhat disfigured by his placement on a seam, his appearance has been improved without heavy overpainting (pl. 24).

Gilded Paneling

The paneling in the Salon Doré is carved oak except for the cornice, the capitals, and the overdoors, which are stucco. The carved areas are water gilded except for the oil-gilded cornice. Although oil gilding is a less time-consuming and less costly method than water gilding, it lacks the vibrancy of water gilding and does not allow for subtle refinements such as burnishing. Out-of-the-way elements that are not accessible to close scrutiny are sometimes oil gilded for the sake of economy.

Restoration of the paneling began in early February 1993. A Parisian firm of woodworkers specializing in antique paneling and frames started by treating the carved wood substrate. The bulk of the woodworking involved filling the holes made in the pilasters by the sixteen electrified sconces. The decision was made to remove the sconces because they detracted from the neoclassical simplicity of the pilasters, but this left jagged holes, roughly 4 ½ inches long by 2 inches wide, in the pilasters. To repair these losses, the holes were evened out to a coffin shape, and flat pieces of oak were cut and glued in each hole. After the glue dried, the flat surface was carved to match the surrounding fluting.

PLATE 25

Northwest corner of the Salon Doré before treatment of the paneling. The trophy panel Music is on the right.

PLATE 26

Northwest corner of the Salon Doré after treatment.

The glue joins on the garlands of the five mirror frames were deteriorating, so the garlands were taken down and treated in the conservation lab. Loose pieces were reglued, and missing sections of flowers and ribbons were recarved in the same manner as the losses in the pilasters. Two small sections of missing cornice were also replaced by casting them from molds made from other areas of the same design. Once it was possible to examine the reverse of the garlands, it became evident that the end swags hanging vertically on the mirrors were constructed differently from the center sections. Probably more recent in origin, they could be either additions or replacement pieces.[28]

On 16 February 1993 five artisans arrived from Paris to begin the restoration of the gilding. They and their colleagues who arrived later in the project spent a total of 8,246 hours over the next eight-and-a-half months returning the gilding to its former splendor. The first step in the process was to clean the gilding, which included not only removing a thick layer of dirt but also removing the varnish and bronze powder paint.[29] In some cases a second, older layer of bronze powder was also found, probably dating to the 1927–28 restoration at the Corcoran. Generally, however, only a layer of a virtually insoluble, red, bolelike material and an overly hard gesso that probably derived from the 1955 restoration were encountered under the bronze powder.

After the cleaning was completed, work began on the gesso, the most time-consuming part of the restoration. Although the restorers' intent was to preserve as much of the old gilding and gesso as possible, the thick red material underlying the bronze powder paint, the hard fill material, and areas of crumbling gesso that were too deteriorated to be consolidated with rabbit skin glue had to be removed first. These areas were sanded and/or scraped to a level at which the gesso was sound or, in a few instances where no sound gesso was found, returned to the wood. In addition, the lower, most visible sections of the two Clark trophies, Theater and Sports, were stripped to the wood so they could be regessoed in preparation for recutting. (These trophies lacked the fine detail of those from the eighteenth century because the gesso had not been recut when they were first made.) It was decided that during the restoration they should be recut to bring them technically and aesthetically more into line with the older trophies. New gesso had to be applied before this process could be carried out.

After sanding and scraping, the problem areas were regessoed. A gesso putty was used for small fills. This putty was activated by moistening it with saliva, a process that led to the startling phenomenon of artisans with ghostly white lips. For larger areas, such as the Clark trophies, the chair rail, and the molding around the window embrasures and on the doors, the gesso was applied as a liquid and built up in successive coats. A head of garlic was added to the gesso for the first coat to increase its tackiness, lending a decided fragrance to the restoration site![30]

After an area had been regessoed, it was sanded smooth, and gesso that clogged interstices and details was cut away using iron hooks. On the Clark trophies the recutter, the most skilled of the artisans in the gilders' workshop, cut details into the gesso over each element of the design (pl. 8). In preparation for gilding the new gesso, a coating of yellow ochre pigment in weak rabbit skin glue was brushed on to cover the white gesso in case the gold did not fill the interstices completely.[31] Three layers of red bole were then applied. At the time of gilding, the bole was dampened and a thin sheet of gold leaf was moved into place and gently tapped down.[32] Areas of gilding to be highlighted were burnished after the gesso had dried. Gold leaf that was not burnished was brushed with a matte coating of rabbit skin glue and water.

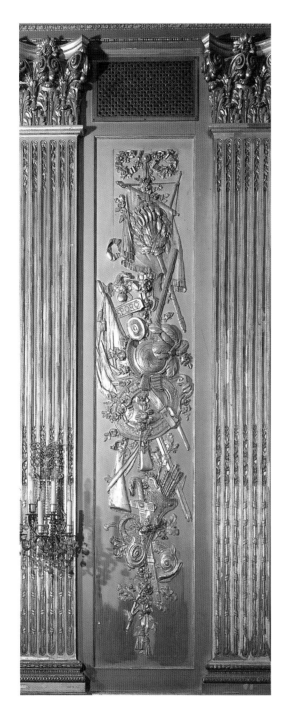

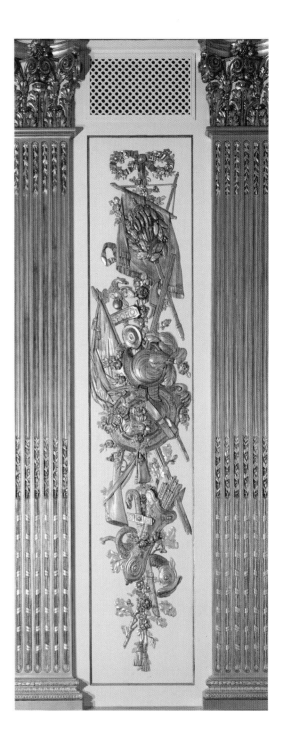

PLATE 27

*Victory trophy panel before treatment. The darker areas of the gilding are
the old gold and the bright are bronze powder restoration paint. The dark
splotches in the painted background are discolored retouching.*

PLATE 28

Victory trophy panel after treatment.

Regilding was also carried out on old gilding that was either incorrect, severely worn, or had oxidized. In the first case, green gold was intended for use only on highlights or secondary motifs. In the New York restoration, however, certain more primary motifs, particularly the flowers on the trophy panels, had been incorrectly restored using green gold leaf. Such areas were returned to their original appearance by applying a layer of yellow gold leaf over the green gold (pls. 13, 14). Regilding in green gold was carried out in areas where it initially had been applied correctly, such as the ribbons on the stop fluting and the leaves of the trophy panels, but the silver in the amalgam had oxidized and darkened the color to an unacceptable degree.

The brightness of the new gilding was then toned down with watercolor to harmonize with the old gilding, which grows darker as it cracks and becomes worn.[33] Normally, new gilding is toned to match the old exactly, but in the Salon Doré it was decided not to tone the new gold to the degree of darkness of the old because the brilliance that is the central feature of a gilded room would then be lost. Instead, the new gilding was toned to the point where it created a unified, overall impression, but on close examination the color difference between the old and new gilding is quite distinct.

Areas on the cornice that required restoration were regilded using a linseed oil mixture as the adhesive. The flat gold bands bordering the floral door panels were also oil gilded, in keeping with tradition, after the background of the flowers had been repainted. Flat wall surfaces were painted primarily by students from the Corcoran School of Art. Since much of the work involved painting around intricate carving, the students were carefully selected for their manual skills and ability to work on a small scale in a precise and methodical manner (pl. 29). A modern oil paint that emulates the color and matte surface appearance of the eighteenth-century *blanc de roi* was used.[34] Utilized in France for historic restorations, this paint was approved by Christian Prévost-Marcilhacy, Inspecteur Général des Monuments Historiques. A small amount of pigment was added to muddy the color slightly and thus make it harmonize with the old gilding. The painting was done after the gilding to create a neat borderline at the interface. Three or four coats of paint were required for adequate coverage. Gilding on the hair and wings of the putti who hold the wreaths over the doors and on the figures of the medallions in the wreaths was painted over because it was a complete aberration.

Painting conservators removed dirt and overpaint from the decorative paintings on each side of the protruding chimney and repainted the white background. The gilded bronze hardware on the doors and windows was cleaned and then lacquered to prevent the corrosion that naturally occurs from the base metal as the gold becomes worn.[35] When the hardware was reinstalled, the position of the door locks was moved from below to above the center painted panel. This was done on the advice of Monsieur Prévost-Marcilhacy, who is of the opinion that the locks would have been at the higher level in the eighteenth century.

PLATE 29

Amy Farina, a student at the Corcoran School of Art, painting the cornice.

Conclusion

The perhaps controversial decision was made not to return most of Senator Clark's furnishings to the Salon Doré. Admittedly, the argument could be made that if Senator Clark's reconfiguration of the paneling is accepted as a reflection of his tastes and era, certainly the room with his furniture makes an even stronger statement. A number of considerations came into play, including the desire to allow the public to circulate freely through the room and closely observe the fineness of the carving and gilding. In addition, in the eighteenth century furnishings such as the corner tables were placed squarely against the wall, complementing and continuing the design of the paneling below the dado rail (pl. 43). Senator Clark's furnishings are a disparate group of objects unrelated to and detracting from the paneling, which is in fact the more important work of art. (From time to time Senator Clark's furnishings from the Salon Doré are exhibited in the galleries with his French paintings and decorative arts.) Furthermore, the suite of chairs and sofas are somewhat compromised by the fact that the Beauvais tapestries are mounted on modern frames, and pieces such as the commodes would not have been part of a *salon de compagnie,* a room for entertaining guests. Rugs were also never a permanent feature of rooms in eighteenth-century France.

Although it is not possible to return the Salon Doré to its appearance in the hôtel d'Orsay, it was our desire to present it in such a way that the artistry of the paneling and ceiling mural might be understood and appreciated. Hopefully the corner tables will eventually become part of the collection, and other tables and chairs that were included in the original design can be identified. Although the paneling stands alone as a work of art, its visual and historical effect would be heightened by the furniture designed to complete its decorative scheme.

The crimson damask drapes described in the inventory of 1774 would also bring the room closer to its appearance when it was owned by the comte d'Orsay and later by Senator Clark. In New York the windows were covered with several layers of fabric, which are now too fragile to be used. The current presentation, although pleasing in its architectural purity, would not have been sought by any of the Salon Doré's creators. Furthermore, the arch of the present windows from Senator Clark's house breaks the symmetry that was established in the hôtel d'Orsay by giving both the large wall mirrors and the windows straight tops with rectangular corners.[36] The architect of Senator Clark's Salon Doré understood the original design and installed curtains whose horizontal tops followed the pattern established by the mirrors and even included some sort of garlands (now disappeared; pl. 7). Curtains with straight tops and swags designed by Chalgrin, the architect of the Salon Doré, for another *salon de compagnie* (1781) seem to offer the perfect solution for the Corcoran (fig. 18).

The room has been known by many names in the twentieth century. It was primarily called the "grand salon" in Senator Clark's house, but it was sometimes referred to as the Fragonard Room because the ceiling was at one time believed to have been painted by the French artist Jean-Honoré Fragonard (1732–1806). In its early days at the Corcoran, the room's official name was the Louis XVI Salon. At some point it acquired the more generic name of "French Room," which it carried until the recent restoration, when it was discovered that in the hôtel's inventory, dated 2 March 1794, the room was called the Salon Doré. We have chosen to retain this historic name as befitting this sumptuous gilded room.

PLATE 30

Trophy panel depicting Arts and Sciences

PLATE 31

Theater trophy panel made for Senator Clark.

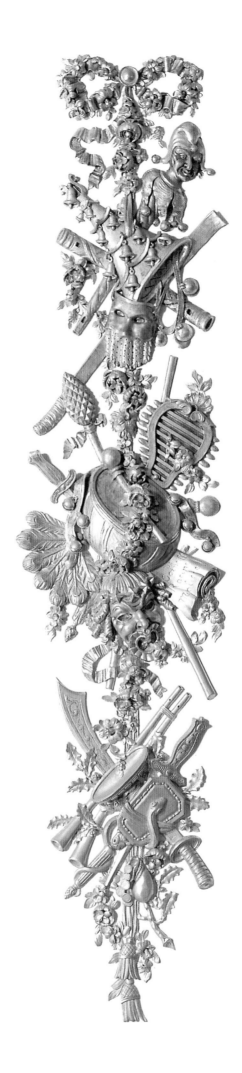

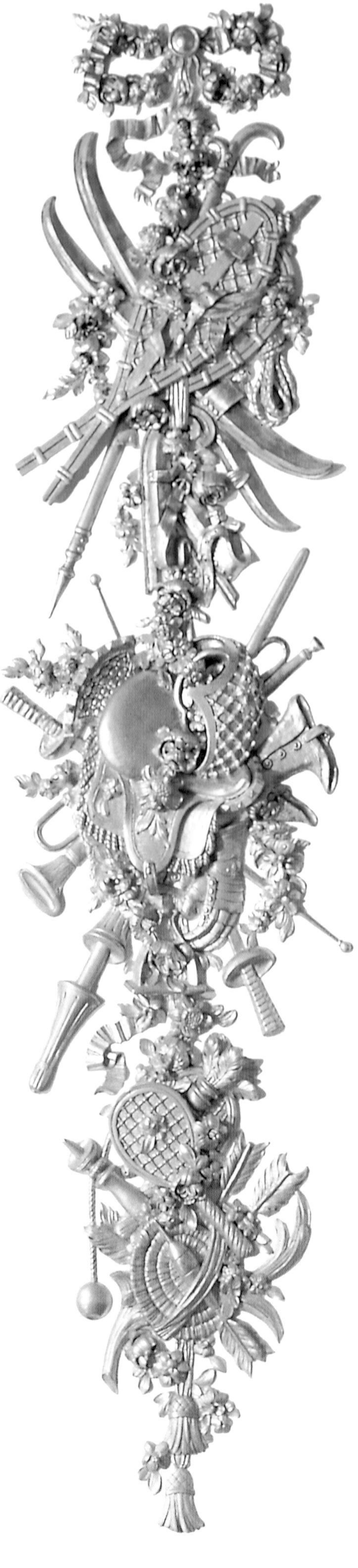

PLATE 32

Sports trophy panel made for Senator Clark

PLATE 33

Trophy panel depicting Music.

1   *New York Times*, 31 May 1908, sec. V, p. 5.

2   *New York Times*, 11 December 1901, p. 8.

3   *New York Times*, 6 February 1899, p. 7.

4   This description of the Clark mansion is culled from the following sources: *Catalogue of Objects of Fine Arts & Other Properties at the home of William Andrews Clark 962 Fifth Avenue*, in the Archives of the Corcoran Gallery and School of Art (hereafter CGSA Archives); photographs made after Senator Clark's death of the interior of the house, also in CGSA Archives; *New York Times*, 28 February 1904, sec. III, p.1; *New York World*, 24 September 1905, magazine section, pp. 6–7; *New York Times*, 31 May 1908, sec. V, p. 5; *New York Herald Tribune*, 6 February 1927, sec. III, p. 3; and *Architecture* 16, no. 3 (15 September 1907), pp. 157–59 and pls. LXXVI–LXXXI.

5   Bruno Pons, *French Period Rooms 1650–1800* (Dijon: Editions Faton, 1995), pp. 102–103.

6   Director's correspondence file, CGSA Archives, box 1, folders 34 and 35. Obituary of Anna Evangeline La Chapelle Clark, *Washington Post*, 13 October 1963, B7.

7   *New York Times*, 28 February 1904, sec. III, p. 1, and 31 May 1908, sec. V, p. 5.

8   *New York Times*, 28 February 1904, sec. III, p. 1. Also *New York World*, 24 September 1905, magazine section, pp. 6–7, when the reporter apparently saw the salon installed.

9   See Bruno Pons, "The Hôtel d'Orsay in Paris" in this publication.

10   *New York Times*, 31 May 1908, sec. V, p. 5.

11   I am indebted to Paul Miller of the Preservation Society of Newport County for information about Jules Allard. For the salon from the hôtel Mégret Sérilly see Pons, *French Period Rooms*, pp. 372–78.

12   See *Catalogue of Objects*. Except for the candelabra on the mantel, all the furniture and decorative arts are now in the collection of the Corcoran Gallery of Art.

13   A group of cross sections was prepared and analyzed by Amy Snodgrass, Associate Conservation Scientist, Straus Center for Conservation, Harvard University Art Museums. Component materials were identified by SEM-EDS and BS, FT-IR microspectroscopy, and polarized light microscopy. Another group of cross sections was prepared and analyzed by Eugena Ordonez (a private conservator in New York) using histochemical stains/fluorescent dyes with reflected light microscopy. Particles taken from the cross sections were studied with transmitted polarized light microscopy, SEM-EDS, and x-ray diffraction.

14   Director's correspondence file, CGSA Archives.

15   At one time the painting was believed to have been painted by Jean-Honoré Fragonard.

16   Charles A. Platt to F. Sampietro, 8 March 1928. Charles A. Platt to T. D. Wadelton, 20 April 1928. Sampietro was paid for "decorative painting," "decorative ceiling," "restorative painting," "gilding," and "glazing"; the latter probably referred to the oil coating. Director's correspondence file, CGSA Archives.

17   Numerous areas contained two layers of bronze powder paint. The uppermost layer dates to a later restoration at the Corcoran (probably 1955), and therefore it is likely that the lower layer was applied by Sampietro.

18   According to Watin in his eighteenth-century treatise *L'art du peintre, doreur, et vernisseur* [The art of the painter, gilder, and varnisher], (Paris, 1975), p. 83, a bit of blue was often added to the white pigment to kill any yellow and make it bright.

19   *New York World*, 24 September 1905, magazine section, p. 7.

20   The actual inscription reads as follows: "Ezt a termet restaurálta (vagyis kizárólag az arauyozást és az ajtókat javitotta) 2 részben (1954 és 1955 évek második felében) PÁLVÖLGYI-PFEIFFER ISTVÁN / okl.gazda, iparmúvész." I am indebted to Victor Szederkenyi of the Embassy of Hungary for the translation.

21   Edward Nygren was Curator of Collections at the beginning of the project. Franklin Kelly was curator from 1988 to 1990. In 1992 Jack Cowart became Deputy Director and Chief Curator, and thus assumed responsibility for the project.

22   The medium was poly(vinyl acetate) AYAC and AYAA 1:1 in ethanol and diacetone alcohol 3:1.

23   Sampling and technical analysis was carried out by Richard Wolbers at the University of Delaware. Cross sections were examined under the microscope in visible, polarized, and ultraviolet light. The primary binder of each layer was identified by staining with direct reactive fluorescent dyes. Pigment identification was done either by x-ray fluorescence or by polarized light microscopy on dispersed samples. Rutherford J. Gettens and George L. Stout give the date for the commercial production of chrome yellow in *Painting Materials, A Short Encyclopaedia* (New York: Dover Publications, 1966), pp. 106–107.

24   The consolidation of the paint layer with gelatin was undertaken by Constance Silver, Moira Duffy, and Shelly Sass.

25   Technical analysis of cross sections from the sky was carried out by Deborah Rendahl and Barbara Berrie of the Scientific Research Department of the National Gallery of Art. Additional technical analysis of cross sections of the painting was also undertaken by Richard Wolbers.

26   According to Gettens and Stout, chromium oxide green, also known as viridian, was first produced by Pannetier, a Parisian colormaker, in 1838 (p. 173). The opaque version was not available as an artists' pigment until 1862. Chromium green oxide was identified here by SEM-EDS, which does not distinguish between opaque and transparent varieties. The ultramarine in the repaint could be the synthetic form, which also dates to the nineteenth century, probably around 1830 or soon thereafter (p. 165).

27   Acryloid B-72 in xylene and toluene 2:1 with a small amount of microcrystalline wax was rubbed on the ceiling with cheesecloth. Retouching was carried out with dry pigment ground in poly(vinyl acetate) AYAC and AYAA 1:1 in ethanol and diacetone alcohol 3:1. A final coating of MS2A in Stoddard Solvent with Tinuvin 292 and a small amount of microcrystalline wax was brushed over the sky and putti to even out the gloss.

28   This is the opinion of Christian Prévost-Marcilhacy, Inspecteur Général des Monuments Historiques.

29   The oil-gilded cornice and flat, painted surfaces were cleaned with an alkaline oil soap. The water gilding was cleaned with rabbit skin glue and/or a solvent gel. Areas cleaned only with gel were afterwards brushed with rabbit skin glue for consolidation. The red, bolelike material underneath the bronze powder paint did not respond to solvents.

30   The gesso was made of rabbit skin glue and a chalk called *blanc de Meudon*. To ensure proper adhesion, a coating of rabbit skin glue and garlic, with only a small amount of chalk for visibility, was applied first. As successive coats of gesso were applied, the strength of the glue decreased as the amount of the chalk increased. Garlic was not used after the first coat.

31   For the two Clark trophy panels the yellow ochre was sponged off the broad surfaces because it makes the gesso too hard for burnishing. The yellow ochre was left as applied for areas of restoration on the pilasters and other trophy panels.

32   The bole used was LeFranc and Bourgeois' *Assiette à Dorer*. For gilding on partial losses filled with gesso putty, the bole was brushed with water containing a little glue. Only water was used for completely new gesso.

33   LeFranc and Bourgeois Designer Gouache in water was brushed on and then dabbed off with a rag. Other techniques were also used to simulate a slightly worn appearance and to blend the demarcation between the old and new gilding.

34   *La Seigneurie Superprimat blanc* oil paint made in France was used.

35   The hardware was coated with Incralac with benzotriazole corrosion inhibitor.

36   See p. 22 of Bruno Pons's article in this publication.

PLATE 34

Detail of the central group of putti in Taraval's ceiling mural, after treatment. The putto on the left was used as the model for the body

of the damaged putto in plate 15.

CONSERVATORS & ARTISANS

*The Corcoran Gallery of Art is grateful to the following conservators and artisans
who carried out the restoration of the Salon Doré:*

Painting conservators
Dare Myers Hartwell

Rachel Benjamin
Cornelia Gill
Helen Mar Parkin
Elizabeth Parr
Catherine Rogers
Marlene Worhach
Rosamond Westmoreland

The conservators were assisted by:
Pamela Downing Adkins
Joseph Hartwell
Jill Westmoreland

Ateliers Fancelli - woodworkers
Denis Lienard

Ateliers Robert Gohard - gilders
Robert Gohard
Fabrice Gohard

Hervé Gehler, *worksite supervisor*
Jean Pierre Bouju
Gwenaël Bourse
Florent Bruneau
Isabelle Dreyer
Philippe Equy
Martine Forget
Romain Gamet
Yves Pasco
Bénédicte Rousselot

Wall painters
Maria Carr
Kaare Chaffee
Amy Farina
Nicole Gallo
Gamble Madsen
Jeff Mays
Julie Solz
Jill Westmoreland

Objects conservator
Meg Loew Craft

Video documentation
Michael B. Sassani
Matt Dibble and Linda Lewett

FACING PAGE
PLATE 35
Detail of the ceiling mural.

The Montana Senator
Who Loved France

ANDRÉ BAEYENS

During my childhood in California, I would sometimes overhear the grown-ups talk about "the Senator." My mother, my aunts, and their friends would invariably turn to me and say, "The Senator so loved France," which I took to be a compliment to my nationality. Only later in my teens did I understand that "the Senator" was my great-grandfather, William Andrews Clark. The eldest daughter of his eldest son was my mother, who, although born in San Mateo, California, had married a Frenchman. It was not such an unusual occurrence at the time.

Since the end of the nineteenth century, and after the legendary earthquake of 1906, San Francisco had grown rapidly. The city's leading families, perhaps encouraged by their counterparts in New York, looked to France as a source of a certain cultural elevation that was somewhat lacking in the boom days of the Barbary Coast. In their quest for the "finer things in life"—a quest that Clark's life exemplified—many successful parents sent their children to France to study its language and its civilization. And so, in the natural course of events, my mother went to Paris, studied at the convent school of *Les oiseaux* (The Birds), and met her future husband.

Although the Senator had passed away before my parents' wedding in Paris, there is little doubt that he would have been delighted by their marriage, for he had indeed loved France. His love was a strong, constant element of his life. The artistic expression of this attraction can be seen in the Corcoran Gallery of Art, where he bequeathed the paintings and *objets d'art* he had acquired in France during his many trips through that country.

Unfortunately, very little is known of the exact dates of his trips, the details of the cities and sites he visited, or, more intriguingly, what there was in France that exerted such a strong hold on a man from Montana and drew him again and again to that foreign land.

On examining different accounts of his life—some favorable, others less so—we can safely assume that the Senator's sojourns in France took place during two separate times in his life. The first coincided with the years of his marriage to Katherine Stauffer, my great-grandmother, who, like Clark, was born in Connellsville, Pennsylvania. One account of the Senator's life states that he first went to France with Katherine in 1878, and shortly thereafter his wife and four children resided in France, acquiring a "thorough knowledge of the French language."[1]

After three years in France, the family moved to Dresden for two more years to acquire an equivalent education in German. Clark repeatedly crossed the Atlantic, spending the winters with his wife and children, and often staying at the hôtel Athénée on the rue Scribe in Paris, near the Opera. From my mother I learned that my grandfather "Charlie" Clark also spent many years of his later life in Paris, a city he loved as much as his father.

In the 1880s Clark acquired works by Corot, Cazin, Millet, and other artists of the Barbizon school from prominent art dealers in Paris, such as Durand Ruel, Boussod and Valadon, and Georges Petit. At this point the question arises: why did Clark prefer these relatively high-priced paintings (10,000 to 20,000 francs, or $2,000 to $4,000 in that period) to those of the Impressionists, whose works were sold at auction in 1878 for as little as 583 francs ($117) for a Manet and 184 francs ($37) for a Monet? I will try to answer that question in the course of this voyage through time.

The second period of Clark's travels to France started after his wife's death in 1893 and his marriage to Anna Eugenia La Chapelle in 1901, the year he was elected to the United States Senate. Before their marriage, Anna, of French-Canadian parentage, had lived in Paris, where she studied languages and music. Under her influence, Clark started learning French in his late fifties. (It was later said that he spoke the language quite correctly, but with an accent.) They were married in France, and their two daughters were born on French soil. Clark rented an apartment in a pleasant area not far from the Bois de Boulogne, the great wooded park on the western edge of Paris.

During the first years of the new century, Clark planned and built his great house on New York's Fifth Avenue. His new residence was designed by Henri Deglane, the renowned architect of the Grand Palais in Paris. Many works of art and furnishings were acquired at this time, including the Salon Doré. This was the most spectacular example of Clark's new interest in works of a more classic age, with those by the Old Masters being particularly important to him. At this time he also commissioned my own childhood favorite: the six lovingly rendered paintings by Boutet de Monvel that depict the life of Joan of Arc, who became the symbol and patron saint of France.

In New York, Clark often used his house and art collection to further French cultural activities. He organized small exhibitions of his French paintings at the Lotos Club. In January 1913, he hosted a lecture under the auspices of the French Institute on "The

Influence of Titian on French Art." By 1916, he was a member of the Institute's Executive Committee.

In the years preceding the Great War of 1914–18, and probably after he had served out his term in the Senate, Clark spent his summers in France with his second family. They often returned to the lower valley of the Seine, between Paris and the Channel coast. This was the favorite haunt of the Impressionists. Clark, however, continued to eschew their works, although in a color photograph taken of him wearing a "boater" under the noonday sun in a Giverny-like landscape (pl. 37), he looked very much like a figure from a painting by Monet. Legend has it that in 1912, he and his family almost took the *Titanic* to return to New York.

After World War I, and before his death in 1925, the Senator continued to be counted among France's closest friends in New York. On 13 April 1921 he attended a dinner organized by the French-America Society in honor of René Viviani, former French prime mimister and special envoy to President Warren G. Harding. And in 1922, he returned to Paris for the last time. We know that during his stay, the Senator visited the tomb of the Unknown Soldier, under the Arc de Triomphe. For him it must have been a profoundly moving moment. We can only wonder, if he felt—or knew—that the country he had enjoyed so much had, like the rest of Europe, changed irrevocably.

Clark's Fascination with France

Clark's life in France began a few years after the end of the Franco-Prussian War of 1870–71. Arriving in Paris for the first time, he found a city that had just overcome the tragedies of that war, nineteen weeks of siege, and the brutal insurrection and repression of the Commune. Despite this harsh reality, the image of Paris remained for many Americans that of the frivolous and almost hysterical gaiety of the Second Empire. Indeed, the future senator was said by his political enemies to have been attracted to the seamier side of Parisian life.

Living with his families in France between the late 1870s and the outbreak of the First World War, Clark witnessed a different and quite decisive moment in the history of the country, one that balanced the development of a modern democratic and industrialized society with the survival of a conservative rural way of life. In the last two decades of the nineteenth century, industrialization was vigorously pursued in France. Considerable amounts of steel, machinery, and railroad stock were produced, and many modern banks were founded. France's technical knowledge was displayed in the Paris World's Fairs of 1889 (for which the Eiffel tower was built) and 1900. In the scientific field, Louis Pasteur developed the first anti-rabies serum in 1885, and Pierre and Marie Curie started studying radioactivity in 1896. The first automobiles appeared, with 3,000 autos in France by 1900 and sixty times that many by 1914.

At the same time, a series of fundamental laws enacted in 1881 and 1882 consolidated the new Republic's constitution and guaranteed the rights of French citizens to assemble freely (thus opening the way to the creation of trade unions) and to have access to a free press. In 1906, Church and State were finally separated by law.

These events could hardly have gone unnoticed by Clark's inquisitive mind, but how he reacted to them is not known. He would certainly have compared them to the evolving politics of the United States and the territory of Montana as it approached statehood. He must have considered the new social laws of France in light of his own industrial experience in Butte, but this aspect of French life most likely did not appeal to him as much as the age-old life of the countryside, with its vines, fields, and villages dating back to the Middle Ages and beyond to Gaul and the Roman Empire. His choice of landscapes and farming scenes for his collection of French paintings, and his later enjoyment of the placid banks of the Seine, testify to his preference.

Interestingly, the industrialization of France during those years did not affect the agricultural population of the country. The urban manufacturing centers were first manned by artisans and shopkeepers from the small provincial towns. Protected by high tariff walls, the farming population continued to thrive, actually gaining a million-and-a-half people from 1870 to 1914. At the same time, only 13 percent of the French population lived in towns of 100,000 or more inhabitants. Sixteen such towns were in France, compared to forty-five in Germany and forty-seven in Great Britain. When the *Grande guerre* began, the bulk of the French army was conscripted from the countryside: farmers defending their land.

The rural areas of France thus retained a traditional way of life well into the twentieth century. They began to benefit from the Republic's laws, in particular those regarding education. The *préfêts* and *sous-préfêts,* local representatives of the central government, actively promoted the integration of the farming communities into the Republic. The *gendarmerie,* a respected constabulary under military command, upheld the new laws outside the urban areas.

It may be true, as Aaron Sheon wrote in the 1978 catalogue celebrating the fiftieth anniversary of the Clark collection at the Corcoran, that turn-of-the-century American art collectors "wanted to collect the tranquil landscapes as objects of meditation, a vicarious means of escaping the social and political issues they faced in their daily lives." Mr. Sheon added: "Their collections permitted them to have contact in their city dwellings with pastoral rural settings, filled with picturesque windmills and hardworking morally sound peasants. Such peasants contrasted with the strikers and anarchists in the American labor movement. In the 1890s, the American Federation of Labor, led by Samuel Gompers, was expanding its influence. There were many strikes during the great depression of that decade."[2] During that decade, Clark was engaged in developing his new venture, the United Verde copper mines in Jerome, Arizona. Perhaps he did derive solace from his Barbizon paintings during the difficult moments that invariably accompanied his large industrial endeavors.

Was that why Clark ignored works by the Impressionists? Hardly, for their peaceful scenes could just as well have soothed his brow, but as a self-made man discovering the art of France, he probably preferred buying paintings by well-established artists with a definite market value, rather than works by unknown and radically different painters.

In perusing Henry James's travel writings *On the Continent*, I came across the following appraisal, written in 1876, of the Channel port of Etretat, a place of gravel beaches and cliffs of white chalk pierced by sea-carved arches. The little town was highly favored by artists, especially Claude Monet. Clark may well have visited Etretat during one of his summer holidays along the Seine.

> *From a Parisian point of view, Etretat is certainly primitive, but it would be affectation on the part of an American to pretend that he was not agreeably surprised to find a "summer resort," in which he had been warned that he would have to rough it, so elaborately appointed and organised. Etretat may be primitive, but Etretat is French, and therefore Etretat is "administered."*[3]

There, I believe, lies the key to Clark's fascination with France. It was not necessarily the landscape—Montana does very well in that respect—but it was how the golden countryside of Normandy and the Ile de France, in the last summers before the Great War, was "administered." This society, structured by laws, with governmental protection and assistance close at hand, encouraged a way of life that had survived the centuries.

As a senator from a very underpopulated and relatively isolated state, Clark may well have seen in France a model for the future political and administrative development of Montana, and indeed of all the western states then entering the Union. My great-grandfather drew assurance from the French example of how settlers newly arriving in Montana would, given time, organize their surroundings and arrange their affairs.

If this was not the case, who can say otherwise? At any rate, it is a happy thought, a token of affection from a Frenchman to his American ancestor.

1   Typed copy of a turn-of-the-century article in the author's possession, perhaps from a commemorative publication.

2   Aaron Sheon, "Nineteenth-Century French Art in the Clark Collection," in *The William A. Clark Collection: An exhibition marking the 50th Anniversary of the installation of The Clark Collection at The Corcoran Gallery of Art, Washington, D.C.* (Washington, D.C.: The Corcoran Gallery of Art, 1978), p. 120.

3   Henry James, *The Collective Travel Writings: The Continent* (New York: Literary Classics of the United States, Inc., 1993), p. 691.

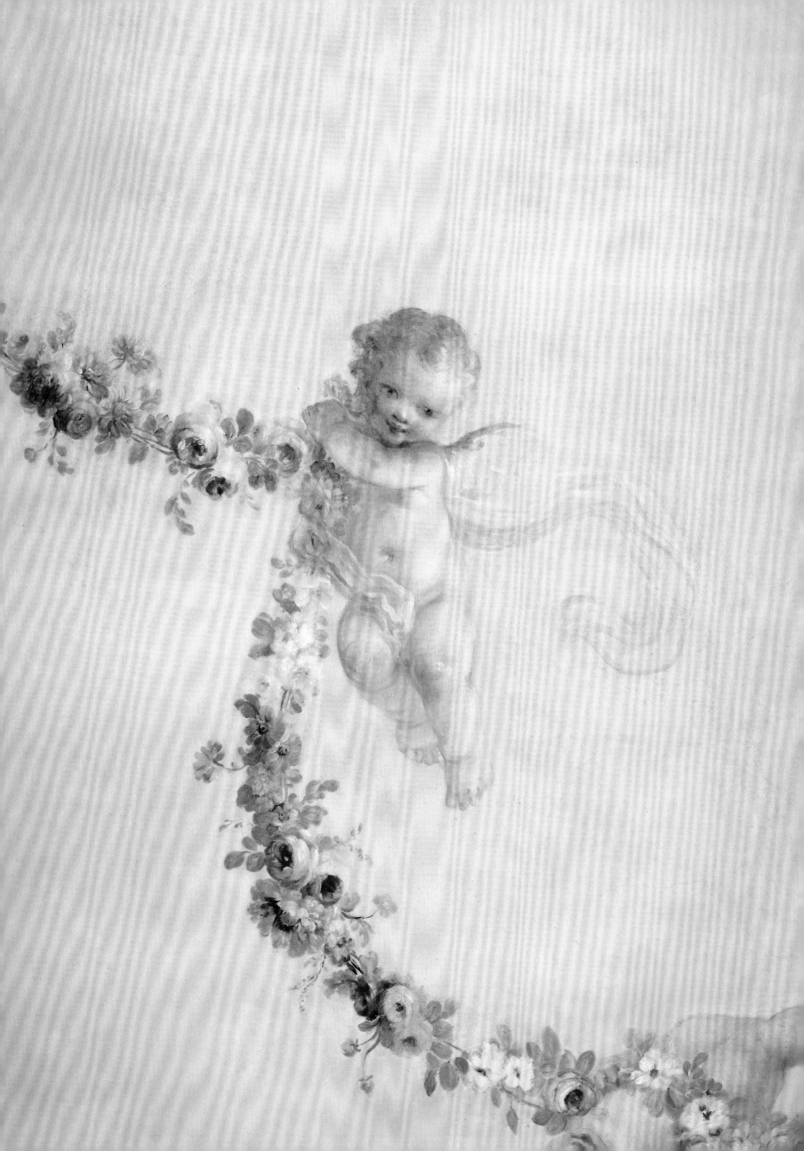

SELECTED BIBLIOGRAPHY

Baulez, Christian. "L'hôtel de Clermont: 69, rue de Varenne." In *Le Faubourg Saint-Germain, La rue de Varenne*. Paris: Délégation à l'Action Artistique de la Ville de Paris et Société d'Histoire et d'Archéologie du VII Arrondissement, 1981.

Considine, Brian B. "The Gilders Art in Eighteenth-Century France." In *Gilded Wood: Conservation and History*. Madison, Conn.: Sound View Press, 1991.

Dumolin, Maurice. "Hôtel Aubry-Vitet." In *Bulletin de la Société d'histoire de l'archéologie des VII et XV arrondissements* (1928): 160–69.

Feray, Jean. *Architecture Intérieure et Décoration en France* [Architectural interiors and decoration in France]. Paris: Éditions Berger-Levrault, 1988.

Hall, Lewis. Introduction to *The William A. Clark Collection: An exhibition marking the 50th Anniversary of the installation of The Clark Collection at The Corcoran Gallery of Art, Washington, D.C.* Washington, D.C.: Corcoran Gallery of Art, 1978. Reprinted in *The William A. Clark Collection: Treasures of a Copper King*. Billings, Mont.: Yellowstone Art Center, 1989.

Le Moël, Michel. *L'Hôtel de Clermont*. Paris, 1978.

Méjanès, Jean-François. *Les collections du comte d'Orsay: dessins du Musée du Louvre: LXXVIII exposition du Cabinet des dessins* [The Collections of the Count d'Orsay: drawings from the Louvre museum: LXXVIII exhibition of the drawing collection]. Paris: Ministère de la Culture, Éditions de la Réunion des musées nationaux, 1983.

Pons, Bruno. *De Paris à Versailles, 1699–1736* [From Paris to Versailles, 1699–1736]. Strasbourg: Association des Publications Près les Universités de Strasbourg, 1986.

⸻. *French Period Rooms 1650–1800*. Dijon: Editions Faton, 1995.

Watin, [Jean-Felix]. *L'art du peintre, doreur, et vernisseur* [The art of the painter, gilder, and varnisher]. Paris: Édition Jacques et Jacques-Charles Chardon, 1755. Facsimile. Paris: Léonce Laget, 1975.

Wilhelm, M. Jacques. "Deux plafonds peints par Hugues Taraval à l'hôtel Grimod d'Orsay" [Two ceilings painted by Hugues Taraval in the hôtel Grimod d'Orsay]. In *Bulletin de la Société de l'histoire de l'art français* (1974): 124–29.

FACING PAGE

PLATE 38

Detail of the ceiling mural after treatment.

AUTHORS' BIOGRAPHIES

André Baeyens

André Baeyens was born in Paris but spent much of his childhood in the United States. Through his Californian mother, née Mary Cecelia Clark, he is a great-grandson of Senator William Andrews Clark. After graduating from the École nationale d'administration in Paris, Monsieur Baeyens entered the French foreign service. He was posted three times to the United States: as second secretary to the French embassy in Washington; as director of the French Press and Information Service in New York; and again in New York as Consul General of France. He also served as ambassador to the Republic of Korea and to the Office of the United Nations and international organizations in Vienna. During his postings in the United States, Monsieur Baeyens lectured and traveled extensively, taking particular interest in visiting the cities and sites where Senator Clark had lived and been active. He currently lives in France and Austria, and he is working on a book on French-American relations that will include a section on his great-grandfather.

Jack Cowart

Jack Cowart, Deputy Director and Chief Curator of the Corcoran Gallery of Art since 1992, was formerly head of the department of twentieth-century art at the National Gallery of Art. Among the major traveling exhibitions and related scholarly catalogues he has organized are the following: *Ellsworth Kelly, The Years in France: 1948–1954; Matisse in Morocco; Georgia O'Keeffe 1887–1986; Henri Matisse, The Early Years in Nice; Expressions: New Art from Germany; Roy Lichtenstein 1970–1980;* and *Manuel Neri, Early Work 1953–1978.* Dr. Cowart received his doctorate in the history of art from The Johns Hopkins University.

Dare Myers Hartwell

Dare Myers Hartwell has been the Conservator at the Corcoran Gallery of Art since 1983 and was in charge of the restoration of the Salon Doré. She began her research on the room in preparation for the restoration, working with conservation scientists and experts in France in an effort to understand the history of the room and to determine the most appropriate course of treatment for it. She was the chief conservator for the restoration of the Salon Doré ceiling mural and the painted floral doors, and she supervised the restoration of the *boiserie* by the French artisans from the ateliers Gohard in Paris. Ms. Hartwell received her training as a painting conservator in museums in the United States and at the Institut Royal du Patrimoine Artistique in Brussels, Belgium. She has a master's degree in the history of art from the University of Minnesota.

PLATE 39

Clock from the private sitting room of Marie-Antoinette at the Tuileries Palace, 1789. Case by Pierre-Philippe Thomire (French, 1751–1843), movement by Robert Robin (French, 1742–1799). Gilded, patinated, and painted bronze, Sèvres porcelain, enamel on copper, and marble. Restored through funds given in memory of Alice Withington Clement, member of the Women's Committee of the Corcoran Gallery of Art.

PAGES 104–105
PLATE 40
Southeast side of the Salon Doré.

PAGES 106–107
PLATE 41
West wall of the Salon Doré.

PAGES 108–109
PLATE 42
Northeast side of the Salon Doré.

Bruno Pons

Until his death in 1995, Dr. Bruno Pons was engaged in the study of the architecture and the decorative arts of the seventeenth and eighteenth centuries. His doctoral dissertation (Université de Strasbourg, 1982) on the ornamental sculptors of the early eighteenth century was published under the title *De Paris à Versailles, 1699–1736* [From Paris to Versailles, 1699–1736]. From 1980 to 1990 Dr. Pons and a team of collaborators undertook research on the hôtels of the faubourg Saint-Germain. Their exhaustive research resulted in seven scholarly catalogues and related exhibitions that were held in Paris. He also examined the architecture of the Rothschilds' residences circa 1880 and wrote the catalogue on the *boiserie* in the Ferdinand de Rothschild collection at Waddesdon Manor in England. His most recent book, *French Period Rooms 1650–1800*, was published shortly after his death. Dr. Pons was both *Conseiller pour la recherche et les relations extérieures* at the Ecole nationale du patrimoine in Paris and an endocrinologist at the hôpital de la Pitié-Salpêtrière.

PHOTO CREDITS

Terry Ashe, pls. 3, 4, 14, 40, 41, 42, front cover
Barbara Berrie, National Gallery of Art, pls. 10F, G
Joel Breger, fig. 29, pls. 15, 17, 19
Giraudon, fig. 6
Peter Harholdt, pls. 1, 2, 18, 22, 24, 26, 28, 30–35, 38, 44, back cover
Hubert Josse, figs. 9–13
Paul Kennedy, pls. 11, 13, 21, 25, 27
Eugena Ordonez, New York, pl. 10D
Edward Owen, pl. 39, 43
Amy Snodgrass, Harvard University Art Museums, pls. 10A–C
Richard Wolbers, University of Delaware, pl. 10E
Wurtz Brothers, figs. 21–27

FACING PAGE

PLATE 43

Northwest corner of the Salon Doré. The table, one of four made for the Salon Doré, is on loan to the Corcoran Gallery.

PAGE 112

PLATE 44

Detail of the Salon Doré trophy panel depicting Victory.